# HOW TO Start a Law Firm When You're Broke

Lauren A. Eagan

AMERICAN BAR ASSOCIATION
Tort Trial and Insurance Practice Section

Cover design by Jill Tedhams/ABA Publishing



Printed in the United States of America.

24 23 22 21 20 5 4 3 2 1

**Library of Congress Cataloging-in-Publication Data**

Names: Eagan, Lauren A., author.
Title: How to start a law firm when you're broke / Lauren A. Eagan, Esq.
Description: Chicago : American Bar Association, 2020. | Includes index. |
Summary: "This book is designed to walk you through every step of starting a law firm-the right way, and without breaking the bank"—Provided by publisher.
Identifiers: LCCN 2019059064 (print) | LCCN 2019059065 (ebook) |
ISBN 9781641056472 (hardcover) | ISBN 9781641056489 (epub)
Subjects: LCSH: Practice of law—United States. | Law firms—United States. |
Solo law practice—United States. | New business enterprises—United States.
Classification: LCC KF300 .E24 2020 (print) | LCC KF300 (ebook) |
DDC 340.068/1—dc23
LC record available at https://lccn.loc.gov/2019059064
LC ebook record available at https://lccn.loc.gov/2019059065

Discounts are available for books ordered in bulk. Special consideration is given to state bars, CLE programs, and other bar-related organizations. Inquire at Book Publishing, ABA Publishing, American Bar Association, 321 N. Clark Street, Chicago, Illinois 60654-7598.

www.ShopABA.org

*To my husband, Ryan Eagan. Without your constant support, Eagan Immigration and this book would be a distant dream. Thank you for always having my back, even when my business and life decisions nearly give you a heart attack. I couldn't ask for a better partner.*

# Contents

Appendices and other resource materials can be viewed here: https://ambar.org/startalawfirm

# About the Author

Lauren A. Eagan, Esq. is an award-winning immigration attorney with multiple offices across the United States. Ms. Eagan attended the University of San Diego School of Law, graduating in 2011. After passing the California Bar Exam, she worked as an associate attorney at private immigration law firms in San Diego, California. As an associate attorney, she exclusively handled immigration law cases, with a focus on deportation defense and humanitarian cases. In October 2014, she left San Diego and moved to Washington, DC.

Ms. Eagan opened her firm, Eagan Immigration PLLC, in late 2014, two weeks after moving to Washington, DC. At that time, she did not have any clients and had spoken to only a handful of attorneys in the area. She truly started her firm from nothing. Over time, and with much hard work, her firm has grown significantly. After only two years, Ms. Eagan opened a second office in Virginia. In 2017, she opened a third office in Washington State.

Ms. Eagan firmly believes that all attorneys have what it takes to create their perfect law firm—one that will allow them to practice the type of law they love, enjoy flexibility and work-life balance, and earn a very comfortable income. All it takes is creativity, strategy, and diligence. Ms. Eagan enjoys encouraging law firm owners from the moment they start thinking about opening a law firm until years after they take the leap.

In addition to constantly working on growing and perfecting her law practice, Ms. Eagan spends plenty of time enjoying life. She loves to travel with her husband and toddler, and has visited more than 20 countries and nearly every continent. Ms. Eagan also enjoys spending time outdoors, and especially loves rock climbing and kayaking. And on cold, winter days you can find her baking with her kiddo or trying a new restaurant with her husband. She rarely works nights or weekends. Ms. Eagan practices what she preaches and always makes sure she has a good balance between her time at the office and her "real" life. After all, what good is all that hard work if you can't enjoy it?

# Foreword

You became a lawyer because you love the law. You care about your clients. You care about your work. Then, you strike out on your own and all of a sudden you have to run a business and you have no idea where to start. You went to law school to become a lawyer, not to become a businessperson. (There's a reason you didn't get an MBA!)

Most of us feel completely lost when we hang our own shingles. And then you look around at all of these other solo practitioners and it seems like everyone has it figured out except for you. Worse yet, you have no income, no idea how to get clients, and your bills keep stacking up.

When I was first starting my law firm and completely lost, I was fortunate to have Lauren as my sounding board. Every time I have had a business idea, I gave her a call, discussed it at length, and gained her valuable input and insight. (Which I still do to this day.) I remember when I did Facebook Live for the first time and called her immediately. I told her that she had to try it. She hopped on to Facebook Live, and from there she worked hard to shape her online presence and has since become a leading authority in the immigration lawyer community on how to leverage social media.

Lauren is a go-getter. I have personally seen her rise from being a broke lawyer to a six-figure earner. This book is a guide that is created from her charging down this path and forging her own way forward. She has laid out each and every step for you so that you can skip the figuring out part of how to run a business and jump straight ahead to earning a great living and doing life-changing work. Lauren will help you go from being broke to earning more than you ever could by working for someone else.

My challenge to you is to use every resource she provides for you here. She gives you actionable steps to take that will skyrocket you out of being broke and into having success beyond what you could have ever imagined. This book is the blueprint that you need and that I wish that I had back when I was lost and trying to figure out how to run a law firm.

Your life and your firm will be transformed by following Lauren's advice. I wish you tons of success on this journey!

Ally Lozano, Esq.<br>Law Firm Business Consultant, Author, *Be the CEO of Your Law Firm: Gain Control, Turn a Profit, and Reclaim Your Life*<br>www.AllyLozano.com

# Introduction

So you're thinking about starting your own law firm? Whether you're doing so because you're tired of answering to a boss, haven't found your dream legal job (or any legal job), or have always intended to open your own practice, congratulations for taking this first step. Starting your own firm is overwhelming, but done right, it will provide flexibility, financial independence, and a thriving career. The best part is, you don't need much money to get started.

This book is designed to walk you through every step of starting a law firm—the right way, and without breaking the bank. Instead of having to wing it, you can follow this step-by-step guide to ensure you don't miss a single critical step as you turn your JD into a successful business. Starting out with a strong foundation will ensure you have everything in place to make your firm last and generate lots of money.

When I first became an attorney, I never thought I would own my own firm. In 2011, I graduated from the University of San Diego School of Law, took the California bar exam, passed, and was suddenly a licensed attorney. Thanks to a position as a law clerk that I started as a 2L, I luckily secured an associate position while still a law student. I resumed work as a law clerk immediately after a post-bar trip to Thailand, and once I got sworn is as an attorney, I got to add that beautiful "Esq." to my name.

I went to law school to become an immigration attorney, and even though I dabbled in other areas of the law as a backup, immigration law is what I love. My first job as an associate was working for a solo practitioner in the immigration law field. I was the first associate this attorney ever had.

My boss was a good man, and he was flexible with my schedule. If I needed to take off for a personal appointment or a last-minute trip, he always allowed me to go, so as long as I stayed on top of my work. But he often fell behind in paying me. I knew it wasn't intentional; he simply lacked the business management skills, and thus the funds, to meet my salary requirements. As a young attorney fresh out of law school with mounds of student loan debt, I desperately needed a steady paycheck.

However, this did force me to learn to network and bring in new clients. I joined networking groups, went to bar association events, and volunteered at immigration-related events in the community. Because I was such a new and young attorney, I did not bring in much business at first, but I learned a ton. All of which served me tremendously when

I opened my own firm, and I will pass this on to you later in the book. But I'm getting ahead of myself.

Just over a year after I began working as an associate, my boss finally realized he could not afford to keep me on as an attorney and let me go. Fortunately, I had seen this coming and was already putting feelers out in the legal community. In the meantime, I took on a couple cases of my own, starting a hastily made law firm with a P.O. box and borrowed office space from an attorney I knew well from networking. Looking back, I'm glad that did not last long, because I was not prepared to run my own firm.

A few weeks after I was laid off, I received an offer to join a well-known and respected immigration law firm in downtown San Diego. I was ecstatic. I was a joining a larger firm, and I would receive a slight pay raise. I looked forward to tackling more challenging cases, working with other intelligent individuals, and having support staff.

The position started off well, and I enjoyed my work. My coworkers were great, my boss made me feel appreciated, and I enjoyed the downtown law atmosphere. Plus, I was learning about so many areas of immigration law that I had never practiced before. I got to spend a lot of time in court, which was a big change from the transactional cases my former boss took. I worked on many different types of humanitarian immigration cases, all of which were new to me. Sometimes, I even found myself running across town to stop ICE from wrongly deporting a client. This was the reason I had gone to law school, and I was loving it.

But about six months after starting, I began to notice some negative changes in the workplace. My boss hired a managing attorney who made me feel micromanaged, requiring me to send her an update every day that outlined all the work I had done. A coworker and I worked out together during our lunch break about three days a week, and one day my boss sent us both a sharp email saying we were no longer allowed to do this. I distinctly remember crying in frustration during one of my annual reviews, and my boss responded, "Don't worry, everyone cries in their review." Even writing that I cried during a review is embarrassing, but to my boss, it was a normal part of the job.

Now that I own a firm and manage staff, I can see where my boss was coming from (except making staff cry in their review—I will never understand that), even though I choose to run my business differently. She was trying to run a business, was probably stressed about the firm finances, and thought that putting pressure on her employees would result in more efficient output and more revenue. I get it, but that environment wasn't healthy for me.

Although I enjoyed the work I was doing, I felt micromanaged and underappreciated, which dramatically lowered my morale and work ethic. I became snappy toward the managing attorney. I lost all drive to work on cases, and my efficiency levels plummeted. If I had an early-morning hearing, I would find an excuse to leave the office early that afternoon, and I spent more time on Facebook than actually working on cases. But I was completely broke, with most of my salary going to pay off my student loans, and I didn't think I had many other options.

In August 2014, my now husband and I decided to make a big change and move to Washington, DC. We had been talking about the move for a while, and I had submitted applications to government positions months before. I began applying for positions with law firms as well, sure I wasn't ready to start a firm myself. By mid-September, I had multiple phone interviews and even a few in-person interviews lined up, and by late September, I had multiple job offers. I turned them all down. I couldn't explain why, but none felt like they were the right fit.

I arrived in Washington, DC, on October 1, 2014, excited. I was sure I would find a job that was the right fit, convinced I wasn't ready to start my own practice. I kept applying for positions in firms and in the government, and again nothing felt quite right. In the meantime, I volunteered at a local nonprofit that handled immigration cases, and I attended networking events and had lots of coffee dates with local immigration attorneys. I was determined to find a good associate position and was pushing hard to get one.

Then, one day, a contact reached out looking for an immigration attorney for a client of hers in Washington, DC. I was not set up to take cases on my own. I did not have a business name, let alone an email address, phone number, or office space where I could meet clients. I hesitated for only a second before responding that I would be happy to take the case.

After accepting the case, I decided to make myself look like a legitimate law firm (we'll talk about how to do this later in the book), and I came up with a name for my firm, got a firm phone number, and reached out to contacts to find a location for an office space. I also researched options for malpractice insurance, refusing to risk liability even for one case. I kept telling myself I would only take on cases while I continued looking for a job at a firm, just to make a little extra cash, and I made sure to keep my costs low.

That first case changed me. There was something magical about working on the case myself, with nobody telling me what to do. After months of feeling micromanaged and underappreciated in a law firm, I was finally liberated. I could handle the case how I wanted. I could come and go as I pleased. Even better, I got to keep the legal fees I earned! I was hooked. I finally got an offer from the firm I had been waiting on, the one I knew would be the right fit, but I was already so in love with having my own practice that I turned it down.

When I started my law firm, I didn't have any money to invest into it. I had just moved across the country and was planning a wedding. Plus, I was still making payments on my student loans. So I knew that if I was going to start my own firm, I had to do it as inexpensively as possible.

I decided that I would never spend more in a month than I earned. I literally started my firm with $0 and invested in it as my clients paid me. Liability insurance? That came as soon as my first client paid her deposit. Business cards? Got those after the first invoice payment. As I got more clients, I was able to invest a little more into the firm, and combined with using free services and carefully managing my expenses, I even started to pay myself. In the first two years of my firm, I never spent more than I earned in a given month.

Now, five years later, my practice is thriving. I easily pay myself six figures per year, and I'm working toward my new, seven-figure goal. I have a small staff who do most of the legal work for me, so I can focus on growing the business. I have won awards for my work as an attorney and have been asked to speak at major conferences. I do the things I want to do and typically work fewer than 30 hours per week in my firm. It all started with the first steps I took to start my firm while completely broke, living in a new city.

Do you want a high, stable salary? What about job flexibility and fewer hours in the office? Do you hope to become well known in your practice area and attract lots of new clients? Well, you could have all of that, with little to no investment. My story is not a fluke. I just did it the hard way, without a clear guide of how to do it. I figured it out along the way and made plenty of mistakes throughout the process. However, my success is based on specific, replicable steps that will help you grow your business, attract clients, and make money with practically no risk. It can work for any attorney willing to put in the work to create a solid, low-cost foundation for his or her firm.

In this book, I will teach you exactly how I started a law firm with no money. I will give you ideas for cheap and free technology solutions for running a practice. I will show you how to get your business started by using online resources, the skills of friends and family, and your own hard work. I will explain all of the business concepts and requirements you need to know to ensure you not only comply with the law, but also run your business effectively. I will outline how to market your business for free to attract a ton of new clients. Most importantly, I will give you the foundation for a successful business that you can grow and mold into your perfect career.

This is your guide to starting a law firm from scratch. Read it, highlight it, dog-ear it, and refer to it often. And, most importantly, take action.

CHAPTER 1

# Making Money While Getting the Firm Started

**OUTLINE**

**Contract Work**
**Document Review**
**Write Legal Articles**
**Work in a Nonlegal Job**
**Chapter Checklist: Get Supplemental Income**

When I talk to attorneys about starting their own practice, the biggest concern they have is about how they are going to make money while the firm gets started. This is completely valid, as we all have bills that need to get paid, lifestyles we want to maintain, and, often, families to support. And to do all of that, we need money, honey. But if that is the main thing holding you back from starting your own firm, don't let it. There are lots of things you can do as your firm grows to ensure you still have enough money coming in to support yourself. While it is stressful to go from life with a steady paycheck to life with no set income, that will not last forever. And honestly, if you follow all the steps in this book, you will likely end up earning way more than you did at a law firm and gain the flexibility and work–life balance you crave.

All that being said, if you're going to start a law firm when you're broke, you will still need to find a way to pay the bills as your firm gets started—it took me about six months to make enough money to cover my firm's expenses as well as my personal bills. Consider erring on the side of caution, however, and plan to wait a full year before earning a comfortable income. It may not take that long, but it's good to be prepared, especially if your goal is to open your firm without investing any personal funds. In the meantime, you will need another source of income that allows the flexibility to work on your own practice. Eventually you will be working for yourself 100 percent, if that's your goal, but in the beginning, you will need to compromise a bit in order to survive. What follows are a few ways to accomplish this.

## CONTRACT WORK

Doing contract work for other attorneys is a great way to make extra money. Many contract jobs allow you to work from home on your own time, so you can get the work done between appointments and casework for your own clients. The only downside is that often the amount of work fluctuates, so you may not always see a steady stream of income. To make your income flow more reliable, you can do contract work for a few different firms or attorneys. This will ensure you have work coming in from different places, just in case one runs out of work to give you or money to pay you. And when you start with a new attorney, find out how much work he or she reasonably expects to give you.

Another option is to find a contractor position for a large firm that always seems to have overflow work, and then tailor your position there based on your financial needs and your need for flexibility as you get your firm up and running. Then, as your firm grows, you can slowly taper off your contract work. A position like this is a great option as it provides more stability, predictability, and a steady paycheck.

When I first moved to Washington, DC, I began doing contract work for former friends and colleagues in San Diego. I emailed attorneys I knew from San Diego who had busy practices, told them I was starting my own practice, and offered to take contract work if they needed someone to draft briefs, prepare filing packages, and do any other remote attorney work. Multiple attorneys responded, happy to have my help. The setup worked out well because the San Diego attorneys did not see me as likely to poach their clients, since I lived so far away, and most of the legal arguments fell under the law of the Ninth Circuit, where I had practiced for years. Because I was familiar with the types of cases I handled on a contract basis, as well as Ninth Circuit law, I was able to research and draft legal briefs fairly quickly. The attorneys paid me on a flat-fee basis, so I did my work quickly and efficiently to make more money per hour and focus my extra time on building up my own firm.

Here are some tips for getting contract work:

1. If you left a position at a prior firm on good terms, talk to the managing attorney about helping the firm on a contract basis. If you know the firm has overflow work in a certain practice area or if you have in-depth knowledge about a particular project or case type, offer to help the firm manage these cases or projects. If they have not replaced you at the firm or trained up your replacement in these specific areas, they may be happy to have you help out as they get adjusted.

   Explain that you are willing to work for them either hourly or on a flat-fee basis per project, and that you will work from home on your own time while adhering to the deadlines they set. If you must go to the office to work on these projects, and that still allows you time to meet with clients for your own firm, that is fine. But if you can and want to work remotely, you can definitely make this part of your terms. If your old firm is hesitant, offer to provide daily or weekly updates on the progress of your work, and remind them that by working remotely, you are saving them money on providing an office space for you. Remember, you are your own boss now, so you can negotiate for the things you want.

For many firms, hiring a former employee as a contractor is an attractive option because they still receive the work of an attorney trained in-house who is familiar with their cases, but they no longer have to pay a full salary or benefits, provide office space, or pay for any "extras," such as conferences, bar dues, staff lunches, and other perks. If the managing attorney is unsure about contracting work out to you, remind him or her of the money being saved on these benefits.

2. Join a social media group that attorneys in your practice area regularly use that might post opportunities for attorneys who specialize in your practice area. Social media connects you to people across the country and around the world, which greatly expands your pool of options when it comes to contract work. Even if you practice state law, you can still prepare work for attorneys in other states or even countries. Those attorneys will just need to review the work to ensure it complies with the laws and regulations in their jurisdiction and then submit it in their name.

   Once you select your social media platform(s), get involved with the groups. Regularly check posts and contribute to the group yourself. Answer questions and provide feedback. This will help you get noticed and position you as a knowledgeable attorney in your field. Regularly search the group to look for opportunities to provide contract work. Try searching *referral*, *contract attorney*, *contract work*, and your geographical location or the name of the court where you handle cases. Eventually, someone might ask for a referral to a contract attorney, and you can offer your services.

   I am part of several different groups on Facebook that are full of immigration attorneys. Many of the groups have a few thousand immigration attorneys from across the country, and some are designed for solo practitioners, many of whom need contractors to help with overflow work. With this many members, there are typically twenty to fifty posts per day in each group, and many come from attorneys who are looking for referrals in other states, or from firms seeking help on a contract basis. In fact, my very first client came out of one of these groups.

   I also joined some more general groups, such as those for solo practitioners, local small businesses, female law firm owners, and mom attorneys.[1] Although these groups are not targeted at my practice area specifically, there is an overlap in the work we do, and occasionally people in these groups need an attorney specializing in immigration law. Once you join some groups relevant to your practice area, see if you can find some additional groups that might cater to your target client. Then, ruthlessly post, respond to questions, and search for opportunities for referrals or contract work.

---

[1] Once I became a parent, a whole new world of networking opportunities that I'd never known about was opened up to me. If you are a parent, take advantage of this!

3. Talk to your contacts. Let your colleagues in the community know you are looking for contract work while your firm grows and that you would welcome referrals. Talk to contacts at large and small firms. Often larger firms get overwhelmed with work on a seasonal basis and look for extra help. In smaller practices, attorneys tend to need help on a contract basis before making the leap to hiring someone full-time. Make sure all your contacts know you are looking for contract work so you are the first person they think of when the need arises.

   On that note, make sure you are actively networking (this book covers networking in more detail in later chapters). Get your face out there. Even if you tell your contacts you are available for contract work, they might not remember if they do not see or hear from you for a while. But if you are out in the community networking and talking to people, they will remember you are available and think of you when they need help.

   There are some specific strategies I employed when networking specifically in the legal industry. First, I got involved in legal organizations, such as the ABA and the local bar association. I attended continuing legal education classes and got involved in subgroups of the organization relevant to my practice. Second, I went to happy hour events where I knew other attorneys would be present. Many of the legal organizations I joined hosted regular happy hours, and so did my law school's alumni association. After meeting attorneys at these events, I usually sent a follow-up email, and if I really wanted to create a business relationship with that person, I set up a coffee meeting to talk more. I then followed up regularly to maintain the relationship.

   Putting feelers out and networking with local attorneys in my practice area is how I scored a stable contract at a large firm. About six months after I opened my practice, an attorney with the largest immigration firm in town approached me at a networking event and let me know her firm was seeking contract attorneys. I contacted her firm and was offered contract work within a week. That became one of my largest sources of income while my practice was still growing; even after my firm grew, I still occasionally did contract work for the firm during slow times. It's nice to have work to fall back on in a pinch, and a large firm tends to have a consistent need for help.

   Right now is the best time to reach out to other attorneys, to network, and to show your face around town. You are just starting your firm and are not overloaded with work, so you have the time to invest in this. And this face-to-face interaction may be your best shot at getting a great contract job and a decent income while you build your business.

All of the options previously outlined are excellent ways to find contract work to provide some financial stability as your firm grows. Try them all. By exploring different avenues to find work, you will find more opportunities, and you will diversify your income stream, which means if someone stops giving you work, you still have work coming in somewhere else. Start putting feelers out, and you may get some work lined up quickly.

## DOCUMENT REVIEW

Similar to contract work, but more general in nature, is document review. This is the process whereby each party to a case sorts through and analyzes the documents and data they possess (and later the documents and data supplied by their opponents through discovery) to determine which are sensitive or otherwise relevant to the case. In a document review position, the attorney typically reviews documents or emails, often from discovery, and organizes and creates abstracts of those documents so that the lead attorneys on the case may analyze each quickly.

Thanks to the advent of e-discovery, most of these documents are digital, so you will probably be able to work remotely. However, some companies working with highly sensitive information require their document reviewers to come into the office. If you need the flexibility of remote work, look for document review positions that fit this criterion.

Depending on your personality, you may really enjoy reviewing information and organizing documents, or you may find the work a bit dry. Regardless, document review provides a steady paycheck, and the positions are fairly easy to find, which is what you are looking for right now. A quick online search for "document review jobs in Nashville, TN" on December 18, 2019, on Indeed reveals 43 available positions. And switching up the search to "document review jobs in Michigan" yields 85 postings. Document review is available around the country, and the jobs are plentiful.

The downside to document review is that it is not the most interesting work. However, it will pay the bills and allow you the flexibility to keep growing your own law firm, which is your main goal. Plus, working in a boring side job will further motivate you to work hard on your own firm so you can earn enough to completely support yourself. Remember, your end-goal here is to start your own, thriving practice, and taking a boring job in the meantime is just one step closer to getting you there.

## WRITE LEGAL ARTICLES

An easy way to make money on your own time is by writing legal articles on a freelance basis. If you are planning to start your own law firm, then you have enough knowledge to be able to write about certain areas of the law. In areas where you have basic knowledge but are a little fuzzy on the details, a small amount of legal research can get you up to speed and give you enough information to write a straightforward article.

Here are a few ways you can get paid to write legal articles:

1. An easy place to find work writing legal articles is Nolo (www.nolo.com). Nolo provides do-it-yourself products to consumers (such as software to fill out your own forms), access to attorneys, and articles that explain different areas and subareas of the law. These articles are intended to be short and easy for the layman to read. Which means you do not have to invest a ton of time into writing a lengthy article filled with legalese and carefully chosen arguments. Simply explain the concepts and requirements in layman's terms.

When first starting my practice, I wrote multiple articles for Nolo about many different subareas of immigration law, and I got paid about $60 to $75 per article. I was usually able to draft a well-written article in about two to three hours, so I ended up earning about $20 to $35 per hour. That's not bad, considering I was able to make that money while sitting on my couch in my pajamas and writing about a topic very familiar to me. Writing legal articles also allowed me the flexibility to work on my own firm, while squeezing in time to write in between projects.

Nolo is a great option for consistent, straightforward legal writing. It keeps your mind sharp and lets you work on topics you are familiar with and enjoy, while still providing the supplemental income you need as you start your business. Plus, you can't beat that flexibility.

2. Another option for legal articles, and freelance legal work in general, is Upwork.com. Upwork is another freelance legal writing company, but it is structured differently than Nolo. Rather than writing educational articles for publishing, Upwork allows users to post requests for legal work.

   To find a job in Upwork, go to www.upwork.com and click on "Find Jobs." Then browse the different categories. Under "Legal" there are several different subcategories, divided up by practice area. If you specialize in one of the practice areas, great! Just click on it and start browsing the jobs. For example, here is a posting listed under the "Contract Law Jobs" subcategory: "Attorney needed to review our current Independent Contractor Agreement and provide feedback, comments, suggestions, etc." The requestor is offering $100 for this service. In another posting, listed under "Criminal Law Jobs," the poster is offering $1,200 to "Test three writers for a month, in seeing who can write excellent Web content on criminal law topics that are outlined for the writer, with primary keyword phrases, and multiple related keyword phrases (to be included) that pertain to the specific pages being created . . . I expect to receive 60 'pages' of content, averaging 400 to 600 words for the $1,200."

   If you have other skills, you can look for jobs in nonlegal fields, such as writing, translation, customer service, or one of the many other categories on Upwork. But if you want to focus on legal writing, there are plenty of jobs to be had. Upwork.com is more like Craigslist for writing, but it is a great way to make extra cash as you start your practice.

## WORK IN A NONLEGAL JOB

*What?! Work in a nonlegal job??? But I just shelled out over $100,000 for my education! Plus interest! I have student loans! My family will think I'm a failure! Locusts!*

Calm down, calm down, you're going to be fine. You're starting your own practice, remember? Who's going to look at your résumé and ask why you worked at the Gap for three months while you were starting your firm? In fact, why are you even putting that on your résumé? During those three months, you were the enterprising new owner of a law firm!

Look, I'm a lawyer, too, and I understand that lawyers typically want to work in the legal field. We often think nonlegal, or at least nonprofessional, jobs are beneath us. It is pretentious and egotistical of us, but many attorneys feel that way. But when starting your practice, you will need to come down from your pedestal and do the best thing for you and your firm. I'm not saying you need to tell your clients or colleagues you bartend every night, but you need to look at this as part of the cost of starting your business. I listed a bunch of legal jobs as options for earning extra cash, but if those don't pan out and you truly want to start your own firm, you need to be prepared to hustle a bit in the beginning.

Even if you work a side job as you get started, keep your legal skills fresh. If you choose to work in a nonlegal job and have the time, consider volunteering at a nonprofit or other organization in your legal capacity once or twice a week. This will keep your mind sharp and can serve as another good way to build your network as your practice grows. And it gives you something nice to tell prying relatives when they ask what you do with your free time.

Now that you've considered a few different ways to make money while growing your practice, you should be ready to take the leap. Many of the things you do to support yourself as your firm grows will give you the much-needed flexibility to meet with clients, work on setting up your firm, and marketing your new law practice. Not having a steady paycheck is often the main reason people hold back from starting their own practice. Speaking from experience, now that I know there are so many ways to make money while growing a law firm, I wish I had done it sooner.

## CHAPTER CHECKLIST: GET SUPPLEMENTAL INCOME

- ❐ **Reach out to colleagues to let them know you are accepting contract work.** Send emails to colleagues. Post on social media where appropriate. Tell people when networking.
- ❐ **Join Facebook groups relevant to your practice are.** Monitor and contribute to the groups daily. Do regular (once per day or more) searches for "referral" and "attorney."
- ❐ **Search for document review positions.** Search on Indeed or another job search platform for document review jobs. Apply to any that make sense for you.
- ❐ **Reach out to Nolo about writing legal articles.** Find out what their application process is and apply.
- ❐ **Register on Upwork and search for freelance jobs.** Search in different categories to see if there are any jobs relevant to your skill set. Apply for any relevant jobs. Set up an account on Upwork so people can find you for jobs.
- ❐ **Search for and apply to nonlegal jobs.** Look on Craigslist, Indeed, or another job search platform for jobs you can do, that would pay you enough to survive, that you could tolerate, and that would still allow you to grow your firm. Apply to any jobs that meet these criteria.

CHAPTER 2

# You May Be a JD, but You Need to Think Like an MBA

## OUTLINE



Some attorneys just want to practice law and don't enjoy the business side of having a practice. But a law firm is a business. While we all went to law school, not business school, you do want to make money from your firm and use it to live your best life. You cannot achieve this unless you focus on the business in addition to practicing law. As the owner of a soon-to-be-successful law firm, you need to think like the CEO of a company, *not* like an associate at a firm.

Unfortunately, law school is geared toward teaching students how to be associates at law firms, but it does not prepare students to run businesses. There are no classes that teach you how to manage the books. There's nothing on marketing for lawyers. And law school certainly doesn't teach you how to hire and fire staff. But for many attorneys, running a business becomes the most important part of their career, if they want to be truly successful and ultimately do the work they love.

This section of the book should be your bible as you start your business. To succeed, you need to lay a strong foundation in your firm, and that is what this chapter is all about. In this chapter, you will learn about business plans, goal-setting, different types of business entities, accounting basics, and tax deductions—all the business stuff you need to run a successful practice. Let's get started with the basics.

## SET GOALS FOR YOUR BUSINESS

Go into a gym the first week of January. It will be packed, full of bright, new sneakers, trendy workout gear, and people excited to burn off the last five years' worth of holiday dinners. Now go back to the same gym sometime in mid-February. How does it look? Likely, the only people there will be the regulars, clearly in shape from months or years of regular exercise. This is an excellent example of the difficulty people have sticking to their goals. A new goal is shiny, fresh, and exciting! You have all the intention of achieving it, but after a few weeks, the excitement starts to wear off, the hard work kicks in, and you realize working toward your goals isn't as fun as you thought. That's when most people quit, and that's why you need a plan.

To get started with your plan, it's time to set some specific goals to help you stay on track. You don't want your firm to look like a gym in February. Goal-setting will allow you to define certain milestones that will ensure your business continues to grow and will help keep you motivated. Without clear goals, it is easy to become complacent and settle back into the status quo. But you're broke, so there's no room for complacency. You need to know exactly what you want and hustle until you get it.

### The Stretch Goal

Now, my husband, an engineer with an MBA, normally keeps quiet when it comes to my business. He has learned that I'm stubborn, decisive, and very independent. One day we had to take a five-hour road trip from DC down to North Carolina, and I really needed to work on my business plan. In addition to being wildly independent, I also get wildly carsick, so my husband agreed to type on my computer while I drove. We started talking about the business, and over the next few hours I learned that maybe it's okay to be less independent and actually take the advice of those with business knowledge. All because my husband introduced me to the Stretch Goal.

On www.mindtools.com, the definition for *Stretch Goal* is "an organizational goal with an objective probability of attainment that may be unknown but is seemingly impossible given current capabilities." In other words, a Stretch Goal is a goal that's really, really hard to achieve.

Setting Stretch Goals is important because they force you to push your limits and dream big. Often, as we're building a business, we get lost in the day-to-day responsibilities, and we forget to step back and look at the big picture or where our firm is going. Stretch Goals help us stay focused so we can achieve them.

### Rewards

If the Stretch Goal is so hard to achieve, how can you follow through? Won't you just end up like the people who stop going to the gym in February? In answer to this question, my husband introduced me to the rewards portion of goal-setting. Rewards?! Who doesn't love rewards?

When setting goals, you should establish a reward to go along with them. Make this something fun and exciting, something you've wanted to purchase for a long time, something frivolous, or something you need but don't have the money to buy until you meet your goal. It can be a big purchase or a vacation you've been wanting to take. It can be an activity you wouldn't otherwise participate in. Make a list of ideas and then narrow it down. You can reward yourself with other items on the list the next time you set your goals.

When you first start out and are broke, it might be easy to restrain yourself from getting the reward regardless of your goal's outcome—because you can't afford it. However, as your business grows and money starts coming in, it becomes easier to obtain your rewards. In order for the reward to serve as motivation for achieving your Stretch Goal, you have to be firm. Enlist help. Find someone in your life who can hold you accountable. You increase the odds of success if you pick out some pretty cool rewards, so you might be tempted to cheat. Don't give in. Use those rewards to motivate you.

## Setting Your Goals

Now it's time to set your goals. My variation on the Stretch Goal resulted in a three-tier goal-setting plan, which includes the Goal, the Stretch Goal, and the Super Stretch Goal. Each is discussed in detail as follows.

When setting your goal in each category, give yourself a milestone that will indicate when you have achieved it. This way you will know exactly when you will receive your reward. Consider using the SMART (specific, measurable, achievable, relevant, and time-bound) goal system. Ensure that the goals fall into each SMART category.

### *The Goal*

For the first tier, set an achievable goal. This will keep you on track with your business and will make you feel good when you achieve it. For example, set a goal to spend no more money than you earn in a given month. Although that goal is difficult, it is achievable and will give you something to aim for.

Under my three-tier plan, you don't get a reward for achieving the goal—other than the reward of personal pride and a positive balance in one's bank account. This first-tier goal should be fairly easy to achieve, so it's not likely you'll give up. However, if you're worried you don't have the resolve to meet your first-tier goal, then assign yourself a reward. It should be something small, but something to look forward to. Maybe dinner out at a fancy restaurant you wouldn't normally splurge on. Or a staycation where you take a couple days off from work. Stock up on fun snacks and go on a Netflix binge.

### *The Stretch Goal*

As mentioned, the Stretch Goal is something difficult to achieve. In February 2016, just over a year into my business, I started using the three-tier goal-setting plan. My Stretch

Goal was to earn $10,000 more in profit (revenue minus expenses) in 2016 than I had in 2015. This was a difficult goal, because I had just started to expand, hiring a legal assistant and contracting out some overflow work. That meant my law firm's expenses had nearly doubled from 2015. Nonetheless, I decided it was possible that I could achieve this Stretch Goal.

This is where it gets fun with the rewards. When I was doing this exercise, I came up with getting my pilot's license, horseback riding monthly, visiting the Minnesota State Fair (it's supposed to be the best in the nation, with every fried food you can imagine), and buying a kayak, among other things. The reward I ultimately chose was a long weekend at a mountain lodge, where I could spend the weekend skiing.

If you're having trouble thinking of a good goal or a good reward for yourself, use the worksheet at the end of this section to brainstorm. Make your goal, and then choose a reward you would truly enjoy.

### *The Super Stretch Goal*

Did you have fun with the Stretch Goal? Well, the Super Stretch Goal might become your absolute favorite. This is something that is technically possible to achieve but you believe is practically impossible. With the Super Stretch Goal, don't be disappointed in yourself if you don't achieve it. The purpose of it is to keep you looking forward, and if you somehow manage to achieve it, you get an awesome, guilt-free reward.

Think about a goal that would be difficult to achieve. For example, do you want a certain number of clients by the end of the year? Do you want to work a maximum number of hours, say 30 per week, while still profiting a certain amount? For me, this lofty goal was to profit at least $100,000 in 2016 (the second year of my business). I profited $62,000 in my first year of business and hired staff in my second year, which caused my expenses to jump, so this goal seemed impossible.

Now, come up with a reward that matches the difficulty of achieving the goal. It should be something you can physically do or afford once you have met your goal, but make it exciting. At the time I set my goal, I still drove the 2001 Honda Civic I got when I was 15. Although I was proud it still ran like a champ at 240,000 miles, getting a brand-new car became the reward for my Super Stretch Goal. Go crazy and have fun with it!

Even though you might not meet your Super Stretch Goal, having a dangling carrot works wonders. It did for me, and I was able to buy myself a new car by September of 2016. If I hadn't met my Super Stretch Goal, I would have survived another year with the Honda and reset my goal for the following year. In other words, not achieving the goal and getting the reward wouldn't have killed me. The purpose of the Super Stretch Goal is to help you stay focused on the larger, long-term goals, while giving you the motivation to meet them faster than you otherwise would.

Now that you've learned about the three-tier goal-setting system, use these worksheets to set your own goals. Don't forget to use the SMART framework to keep you on track!

### GOAL AND REWARD BRAINSTORMING WORKSHEET

| Goal Tier | Goal Ideas | Reward Ideas |
|---|---|---|
| Goal | | |
| Stretch Goal | | |
| Super Stretch Goal | | |

With these ideas in front of you, select your top Goal, Stretch Goal, and Super Stretch Goal, along with corresponding rewards. Look at the worksheet you just filled out and figure out which goals will best help your practice grow in a way that allows you the lifestyle you want. Then decide which rewards will best motivate you to achieve those goals. Fill out your selections in the following worksheet.

### FINAL GOAL AND REWARD WORKSHEET

| Goal Tier | Goal | Reward |
|---|---|---|
| Goal | | |
| Stretch Goal | | |
| Super Stretch Goal | | |

After you select your goals and rewards, integrate them into your business plan. Since you will be reviewing your business plan at least every six months, your goals will stay fresh in your mind. For extra motivation, print them out and hang them where you can see them. The more you are reminded of your goals and rewards, the more you will make choices that will help you achieve them.

As you meet your goals, update them to make your law firm better and better. After you meet a goal, select the next one and repeat the process.

# MAKE YOUR BUSINESS LEGAL

Now that you have a business plan and set goals, it's time to take the first steps toward turning those goals into reality. To get clients, start working, and earn attorney's fees, you will need to take some steps to ensure your business is set up properly and that you're meeting all state and federal requirements as a business owner.

## Decide on a Business Entity

The first thing to do is decide which type of business entity your law firm will be. The options include (but are not limited to) sole proprietorships, partnerships, subchapter S corporations, limited liability companies (LLC), professional limited liability companies (PLLC), and corporations. Outlined in the following section are the advantages and disadvantages of each type of entity. An accountant can help you decide which type best fits your business model.

### *Sole Proprietorship*

Sole proprietorships are the simplest of the entities and have only one member. They are very easy to set up and require little or no filing with the state government, depending on the state where the business is located. On top of that, taxes remain pretty easy compared with taxes done for other business entities, with the profits and losses of the business recorded directly on your tax return.

Although sole proprietorships are simple to set up, the main drawback is that you as the owner can be held fully liable for the actions of your law firm and its employees. This means that if a judgment is entered against your law firm, the government can come after your business assets, as well as your personal assets (think house, car, etc.). It's a simple way to start a practice, but carries a lot of risk.

However, sole proprietorships are easy to set up, so they are a good short-term option for people wanting to open their own firm. The benefit of actually taking the major step of opening your law firm, even when you're broke, outweighs the liability risks. Especially in the beginning, when you and your firm don't have much to lose.

However, do consider changing to a different business entity once your firm grows and you are earning enough money to warrant the extra protection and can pay a professional to help you with the entity switch.

### *Partnerships*

There are several different types of partnerships, each with different levels of liability protection. General partnerships (GPs) offer the least amount of liability protection.

They do not protect against personal liability, which means that if things go south, you could be responsible for every debt the law firm accrues, so they carry a heavy risk. If someone sues your firm and you lose, collectors can come after your personal assets. However, a benefit of general partnerships is that they are simple and typically have no formalities, such as annual meetings, that you must comply with.

Limited partnerships (LPs) have two classes of partners: general partners, who own and operate the business and are liable for its debts, and limited partners, who invest their money in the business, typically do not have authority to make any decisions regarding the operation of the business, and do not have personal liability for the business debts. LPs have more formalities than a general partnership, including a written certificate of partnership and annual meetings.

Limited liability partnerships (LLPs) are basically general partnerships that give at least some limited liability protection to the partners. In some states, all partners are afforded this protection, much like an LLC. LLPs have more formalities than a general partnership, similar to those required by an LP.

The protections and availability of LPs and LLPs differ from state to state, so check your state and local laws regarding these entities. Regarding taxes, all three partnership formations are taxed as pass-through entities. This means that your law firm will issue K-1s to the partners, and the partners will record that income on their personal tax returns.

When it's time to switch entities, consider the LLP. This is the best of the partnership entities, in my opinion. It affords some liability protection to all partners, so their personal assets are protected. Once your firm starts growing, this protection is vital to all owners of the firm.

### *Subchapter S Corporations*

Subchapter S corporations (S corps) are strictly tax elections that the managers of either a corporation or an LLC can make. The benefit of being taxed as an S corporation is to avoid the corporate-level taxation to which corporations are subject. This could lead to a significant amount of savings if your business would otherwise be taxed at the corporate rate. However, S corporations are limited. In order to be taxed as an S corporation, the company must be domestic, have only non-business, non-foreign owners, have fewer than 100 owners, and have only one classification of stock.

If you're considering becoming an S corp, definitely talk to an accountant. This is the tax election I now use for my firm, and even with the help of an accountant, getting all the paperwork properly filed was complicated. However, now that it's all set up, I prefer it to my previous tax status as a sole proprietor. There's too much to get into here, but the most important takeaway is that with the tax election, you will be able to keep more of the money you make.

### *Limited Liability Companies*

Limited liability companies (LLCs) and professional limited liability companies (PLLCs) are unincorporated entities. This means that although they are not incorporated, they are separate entities for accounting purposes. Basically, they are a step between a sole proprietorship and a corporation. Because they are not incorporated, members of the LLC have more rights to run the business than a shareholder of a corporation. However, not all states allow attorneys to run their law firms as LLCs or PLLCs, so make sure to look into this.

The benefit of LLCs and PLLCs is that they allow for more flexibility than corporations, while still protecting members from personal liability. To maintain an LLC, the company is treated as a separate entity, meaning you don't comingle your own finances with those of the LLC. When it's time to file taxes, the taxes will be recorded directly on each member's tax returns, without first being subject to a separate corporate tax.

As previously noted, attorneys who are just starting their firms, especially broke attorneys, should consider a sole proprietorship, as the increased liability from a sole proprietorship is not too worrisome. However, once you start making money and your firm begins to grow, consider switching to an LLC or PLLC. This provides more safeguards and protects your personal assets. Ultimately, after speaking to a business law attorney and an accountant, I chose a PLLC with the S corp election for tax purposes. This combination has reduced both my personal liability and my tax liability, making my business stronger and safer.

### *Corporations*

Of the different business entities, corporations require the strictest formalities. Corporations typically must have shareholders, a board of directors, and a management team. Although you can fill all those roles as a sole owner, you must ensure that you operate in each role separately, keeping careful records to show your conformance with these corporate formalities. You must keep track of meeting minutes for board of director meetings, even if you are the only board member. In most states, you must file an annual report.

The main benefit of a corporation is that there is a separation between ownership and management that protects the corporation's owners from liability. If you plan to grow your business into a law firm with multiple levels of management, a corporation might be a good fit for you. However, there are major tax drawbacks to owning a corporation. By default, the profit of the company is taxed at the corporate tax rate before it is distributed to shareholders (you), who are then themselves liable for taxes on their corporate gains. This essentially means that you will be taxed twice.

Considering waiting as long as possible to switch to a corporation. Honestly, I made the decision not to incorporate when I learned about the intense record-keeping requirements, and frankly, corporations are not necessary for most law firms. Fortunately, if your firm does grow to the point that you need to incorporate, by that time you will be making plenty of money and will have a good business attorney and accountant on your team. Consult them to make an informed decision.

The American Bar Association published a helpful article that included the following questions regarding how to determine what entity is best for you:[1]

- How many owners will you have? If you plan to grow, you either need a strong operating agreement as an LLC; a strong partnership agreement as a GP, LP, or LLP; or a corporation to protect you from potential future liability from co-owners.
- How much is limited liability protection worth to you? Filing fees, tax forms, and annual reports cost money. Sole proprietorships and partnerships have lower operational costs, whereas LLCs have medium operational costs, and corporations tend to have higher operational costs.
- How much money do you anticipate earning? If you anticipate earning less than what you consider a reasonable salary, then there's no real benefit to an S corporation.
- How organized are you? Corporations require recording meeting minutes and annual meetings, all of which are additional layers of formalities to manage.
- Do you plan to ever sell the entity? How do you plan to accomplish that sale? Stock sale? Sale of all assets? Shares are easier and cheaper to sell than the assets of a company. LLC ownership and partnership ownership is less quantifiable, and therefore, it is typically more complicated and costly to sell an LLC or partnership.

Setting up your new practice as a sole proprietor is the easiest, requiring practically nothing. You don't even need an employer identification number to file your taxes. Although sole proprietorship comes with a high risk of liability, you likely won't have much to lose at first. However, as your business grows, you might feel it's too risky to continue without protection from liability and switch to a PLLC, getting taxed as an S corp. This structure leaves you with quite a bit of flexibility for running your business. This is just an example; what you decide to do may look completely different. Use the questions to guide you as you get started.

After you determine which entity you want to use for your business, do additional research into the requirements for setting up that entity. If the requirements make sense to you, go for it. You're broke, after all, so anywhere you can save money helps. But if you feel overwhelmed, try reaching out to a colleague who can guide you or answer questions for free or at a very reduced rate as you do it yourself. You don't want to make a mistake that could affect your firm down the road.

## Register Your Business

Next, you need to find out your state's requirements for a new business. Usually, it is fairly easy to find these requirements by Googling *start a business in [name of your state].*

[1] Richard Bobholz, *Law Firm Choice of Entity,* American Bar Association (Mar. 1, 2015), https://www.americanbar.org/groups/young_lawyers/publications/tyl/topics/solo-small-firm/law-firm-choice-entity/.

Some states, like Virginia, have fairly brief guidelines with links to the relevant forms and websites. Other states, such as Pennsylvania, practically have books outlining the required steps for opening a business. Look at the requirements for your state, and follow them carefully.

In addition to registering with your state, you also need to register with your state's bar. For many attorneys, this will be the state in which you are licensed, but for some attorneys, like me, who practice federal law, this could include state bars in which you are not licensed. To learn how to do this in your state, just search *register my business with the [name of your state] state bar*. You should find links to the exact forms you need to fill out. Easy-peasy!

Keep in mind, you will likely need to pay an annual fee to both your state and your state bar once you register your business. Keep a record of these fees so you can account for them each year.

## Taxes!

After you have registered your business with your state, get set up with the Internal Revenue Service (IRS) to pay your taxes. Go to www.irs.gov/businesses/small-businesses-self-employed or google *IRS Small Business* for a guide on how to get set up, how to pay your taxes, and when to pay your taxes.

Please note that you will need to pay QUARTERLY TAXES. I put that in all caps because it's very important and *none of my friends who own new law firms do it!* I put that in italics because I am shocked and appalled that they would waste money like this. If you don't pay your quarterly taxes, you will get fined when it's time to pay your annual taxes. And since you're broke, you don't like fines.

Anyway, quarterly taxes are taxes you pay every quarter. For the first year of your business, your quarterly taxes are based on the amount of money you anticipate earning that year. For all subsequent years, they are based on the previous year's income. The IRS website has spreadsheets that tell you how to calculate and submit your quarterly taxes. Use them and pay your taxes every single quarter. Google *[current year] federal quarterly tax payments* to find out the due dates for the current year.

After you're set up with the IRS, register with your state and local tax bodies. In most cases, you will find instructions on how to pay taxes in your state on the websites you used to register your business. If you can't find the relevant information there, google *[Name of state] tax board*. Do the same thing for your county and town to ensure there are no local taxes you need to pay. Check the requirements for quarterly taxes with your state and local tax bodies as well.

Taxes can be tricky, and many people get an accountant immediately. Frankly, in the beginning you're broke, so it's pretty simple—use TurboTax. Consider getting an accountant in the future, but for now, take this opportunity to learn how to do it yourself and save some money.

## SET UP YOUR BANK ACCOUNTS

When you start getting clients and making money, you will need a bank account. Unless you're like my friend Rachel, whose only goal is to save as much money as possible so she can retire early in Cancun. Rachel—who, believe it or not, is a really good attorney—has no bank accounts, gets all her money in cash, and stashes that cash somewhere in her tiny apartment so she doesn't have to pay taxes on it. This is obviously illegal, and I wouldn't recommend it. So unless you have big dreams to disappear forever in Mexico, time to get those bank accounts set up. Your firm is going to need the accounts outlined in the following sections:

### Operating Account

Your operating account is essentially the checking account for your business. You will pay your bills from this account, you will take earned attorney's fees into this account, and you will pay yourself from this account.

Consider opening an operating account with the same bank where you have your personal checking account. Even though you will always keep the funds separate, this makes it easy for you to pay yourself quickly. Most banks offer the means of transferring between accounts, thereby saving you time. The money moves to my personal account instantaneously. It's pretty convenient, especially when you happen to be on vacation and realize that you forgot to pay the rent.

There are benefits to getting an account at a Big Bank, especially one that has a location near your office. Sorry to those who are anti–Big Bank, but it's just easier. Often, my clients need to make direct deposits into my account, and it's easier when the bank has multiple branches in order to facilitate making a deposit nearby. And I like having an ATM half a block from my office. When I'm carrying $6,000 in cash, I don't want to walk very far to deposit it. Especially on the mean streets of two-blocks-from-the-White-House. It's rough out there.

### IOLTA

If you think you will be taking client funds AT ALL, you need a trust account, officially known as an interest on lawyer trust account (IOLTA). Some attorneys never take client funds in advance, so they don't have IOLTAs. For others, this is impractical. For example, I often pay filing fees for my clients, and the clients will pay me in advance. I need to hold that money in trust. And I have all my clients pay a retainer, which I do not move to my operating account until I have earned the fees. Honestly, even if you don't think you'll ever hold client funds, open an IOLTA anyway. It's free, it's good to have just in case, and the only thing you lose is a little bit of time setting it up.

Set up the IOLTA at the same bank where you have your operating account. You will make a lot of transfers between the accounts, so you will need to have easy access. Request a banker who has opened trust accounts before. You will thank me later. Finally, you must *insist* that the bank add the IOLTA to your online banking. This can sometimes be a struggle, mainly because bankers might not have experience with this type of trust account. But it is an absolute necessity. You need easy access. You don't want to have to go to the bank every time you need to transfer money from trust to your operating account. If the bank tells you they can't do it, ask nicely to speak to a manager. Ask for a number to call. Call that number until you find someone who can help you. If none of that works, tell them your friend Lauren Eagan did it, so you *know* it's possible.

Once you have your IOLTA account set up, here are a couple of my helpful tips, after years of trial and error:

1. Get checks for your IOLTA account and use them to pay filing fees or refund client trust money. If the bank says you can't get checks for an IOLTA account, DON'T BELIEVE THEM! I did, and it messed up my accounting for years as I transferred money from trust to operating and then wrote the checks out of operating. Once I realized the bank had lied to me and ordered some checks, the nightmare of IOLTA accounting became as peaceful and relaxing as my early morning yoga sessions.
2. Cross-check your IOLTA accounting monthly. Make sure the amounts you moved in and out of the account match up with what you have recorded in all your clients' trust account records. If you wait too long to do this, it will be harder to correct mistakes, so be consistent with this.

Trust me, just do those two things, and your IOLTA accounting will go much more smoothly.

## Savings Account

If you're broke now, you won't be soon enough, young grasshopper. Once you start making money, you want to earn interest like it's your job. While you should use the same bank for your business checking and your IOLTA, it doesn't matter where you bank for your business savings. Just make sure you're getting the best interest rate possible on your investment.

To find a good savings account, start shopping around to different banks and comparing interest rates on savings accounts. There are quite a few lists you can find online if you search "best high-yield savings accounts." I suggest pulling up a few different lists to compare, and then deciding between the options listed on multiple lists. Nerdwallet.com is also a reputable site you can take a look at, although their lists will probably pop up in your search. When you find the best rate, open your savings account there. I ultimately opened a savings account for my law firm with Capital One 360. I got it about five years ago, so the interest rates may be better at other banks now, but I know it still ends up on most of the high-yield savings accounts lists.

Once you open a savings account, link it to your operating account. This way you can easily transfer funds. Typically, transfers between different banks can take a few days, but that doesn't matter with the savings account, since you are leaving money in that account to accrue interest until you need it.

### Line of Credit

Before I start talking about credit cards, I want to remind you that you're broke. And you probably also have student loan debt. You may also have credit card debt. The purpose of getting a business credit card is not to take on more debt. It is to earn benefits for free. Put as many of your expenses as possible on your credit card, but also make sure to pay off your credit card every single month.

This is another account where it may pay to be at the same bank as the operating account. First, banks often waive the bank fee for the operating account if you put a certain amount of money on a linked credit card per month. Second, it will make it easier and more straightforward to pay off your credit card every month. Third, banks often use credit cards to serve as overdraft protection. Check with your bank on this, and set it up if possible.

However, if none of these benefits apply at your bank, shop around and get a credit card with the best deal possible. Look for credit cards that offer cash back or some other reward that is useful to you. I'm originally from Seattle, and my parents still live there, so I travel there all the time. One of the main airlines out of Seattle is Alaska Airlines, which conveniently has credit cards through Bank of America that allow you to accrue airline miles. I got both personal and business Alaska Airlines credit cards, and I use them for everything. This paid for my flights to and from Jackson Hole, Wyoming, this summer using only my airline miles. And I was able to fly my mom to Virginia to dog-sit while my husband and I went to Africa (is my mom the best, or what?).

The point is, get a credit card that gives back. Then, use it for everything and pay off the balance every month.

## GET MALPRACTICE INSURANCE

At this point, you must really be thinking like an MBA. Corporate entities, goal-setting, banking—but we're not done yet! Next on the agenda is to get malpractice insurance. This is an absolute must. If you mess up a case or disagree with a particularly litigious client, malpractice insurance will save your hide. If you are already practicing law without malpractice insurance, get some immediately.

Malpractice insurance can be a bit pricey for a broke lawyer, so wait to purchase it until the day your first client retains you. That way you can pay it off immediately but still have the coverage needed to practice law. Research companies and get quotes ahead of time so that you're ready to purchase it the day you need it.

When looking for a good malpractice insurance company, ask colleagues in your field for recommendations. I use Complete Equity Markets, which was recommended to me by multiple immigration attorneys. The American Bar Association also offers malpractice insurance, and I highly suggest getting a quote if you are a member. If none of those options pan out, a Google search for "malpractice insurance for lawyers" yields quite a few results. Call around and read reviews to find the best option.

For detailed information about malpractice insurance, check out an Above the Law article titled "The Practice: Answers About Malpractice Insurance" (http://abovethelaw.com/2013/01/the-practice-answers-about-malpractice-insurance/). In this article, the author, an attorney, interviews a malpractice insurance broker to get all the details about malpractice insurance. Suck it up and get it. It might seem expensive as a broke, new business owner, but it could save you thousands down the road.

## USE AN ACCOUNTING SOFTWARE TO TRACK *EVERYTHING*

Tracking your firm's revenue and expenses is one of the most important parts of running a business, but sadly, most attorneys neglect to do it. Accounting is something law school definitely does not prepare us for, but it is critical to running a successful business. If you properly track your revenue and expenses, you will see at a glance, how close you are to meeting financial goals. You will find areas where you can cut back and save your firm money. And you will learn about important tax deductions that can save you hundreds and thousands of dollars.

### Cheap or Free Software Recommendations

Another thing to do early on is find a good accounting software that works with your budget. The software should integrate with your bank accounts and credit cards and allow you to track and categorize all income and expenses, generate reports, and create client invoices. And if it allows you to accept credit card payments directly through the software, even better.

The Wave Accounting software is free and very easy to use. It integrates well with all your accounts, and allows you to see your monthly revenue and expenses for up to two years right on the account's dashboard. This lets you see how close you are to meeting your goals. It also makes professional-looking invoices that you can print or set up to email directly to your clients. It generates all kinds of reports, which makes it easy to find problem areas in your practice, such as where you're spending too much money, or to project upcoming expenses. It is an excellent program with an even better price tag.

### Categorizing Your Income and Expenses

Once you select an accounting software, link it to all your business bank and credit card accounts, and set it to import transactions as far back as possible. Since you just started your firm, you probably won't have many transactions yet, but you want to make sure to include everything.

After your transactions are imported, categorize all of them, based on the type of expense—for example, Dues and Subscriptions, Public Transportation, Parking, Office Supplies, Meals and Entertainment, Conferences and Meetings, and Attorney's Fees, Contract Work, and Consultation Fees. Depending on your firm expenses, you may use very different categories than these, but the point is to categorize everything.

Everything in a category? Good. There are two main benefits to categorizing your income and expenses: (1) You stay informed about where your money goes and where it comes from. If everything is categorized, you can quickly generate reports to analyze the state of your business. (2) Tax purposes. There are many different deductions for which businesses are eligible, and you want to cash in on as many as possible. In order to do that, you need to keep your expenses categorized to perfection.

Now that you've categorized your initial transactions, make this part of your weekly routine. Appendix A, "Weekly Tasks," shows how to categorize your law firm's transactions on a weekly basis. Doing this weekly is important for a couple reasons. First, it ensures you have a reasonable number of transactions to categorize at a time, rather than having to go through hundreds. Second, it is much easier to remember transactions that happened a week ago than those that happened farther in the past. If you remember the transactions, you will be able to categorize them quickly, giving you time to work on other tasks. So even if you do not like dealing with the financial side of your practice, get in the habit immediately.

## PREPARE FOR TAX SEASON

If you've never owned a business before, tax season may not bother you too much. Sure, you have to fill out your taxes or shell out some money to have someone prepare them for you, but usually you end up getting at least a few hundred dollars as a refund. It feels like a little bonus in April for all your hard work.

As a business owner, you can kiss that tax refund goodbye. I think my husband may have cried a little in 2016 (our first tax year as a married couple filing jointly) when he realized he was never going to get a tax refund again. Sorry, pal, those days are over. But hey, you have an awesome, rainmaking businesswoman for a wife—worth it!

### Tax Deductions to Track

The good news is that even though you now have to pay taxes in larger lump sums, you get to take advantage of some fun tax deductions. When I first opened my law firm, I attended as many tax seminars, webinars, and lunch-and-learns that I could find for free. I found a lot of them through the state bar, and I recommend you do the same. We will cover some of the best tax deductions, but consider consulting a CPA or accountant who does this for a living. Once you learn about the different tax deductions you can use, carefully track and categorize all expenses associated with those deductions. It will save you a bundle and help turn you from broke to rich.

Here is a handy list of the top tax deductions for a small business:

- **Car and truck expenses.** Since most law firms don't use a vehicle to conduct business, what you're really going to track is your mileage. Record all miles you drive to and from business-related events. If your office is in your home, you will track your miles beginning to and from home and between events, but if you have a full-time office, you can only track miles to and from your office and between events. Which means you can't get reimbursed for the miles it takes you to drive from your home to the office.

  To find out how much you will get reimbursed per mile, google *IRS annual mileage reimbursement rate*. At the time of writing this, the reimbursement rate was 57.5 cents per mile.
- **Salaries and wages.** Payments to employees, including salaries, wages, bonuses, commissions, and taxable fringe benefits, are deductible business expenses for the business. However, payments to sole proprietors, partners, and LLC members are not wages because these owners aren't employees, so if you don't have any employees yet, this section won't apply to you.
- **Contract labor.** If you start using a contractor for overflow work or to help with a specific project, you can deduct the cost of the contract work. Make sure to issue Form 1099-MISC to any contractor receiving $600 or more from you in the year. To make this easier during tax season, ask every contractor to give you a filled-out Form W-9 at the time he or she begins working for you.
- **Supplies.** The cost of items used in a business (laptops, filing cabinets, file folders, postage, etc.) are fully deductible business expenses. Keep track of these things and make sure to categorize them in your accounting software.
- **Rent on business property.** Even if you just rent office space by the hour (which we'll discuss later), you can deduct it. Same goes for a home office if it's your sole office, although you can only deduct a percentage of the rent that is equal to the percentage of space your home office takes up in the house.
- **Utilities.** All utilities are deductible. If you have a home office and no other office, a portion of your home utilities are deductible, too, based on the percentage of space the home office occupies in your home.
- **Taxes.** You can deduct licenses, regulatory fees, and taxes on real estate and personal property. Your employer taxes, including the employer share of FICA, FUTA, and state unemployment taxes, are fully deductible business expenses. However, for self-employed business owners, the deduction for half of your self-employment tax is not a business deduction; it is an adjustment to gross income on your personal income tax return.
- **Insurance.** I know you didn't want to get that liability insurance we talked about earlier but look! It's tax deductible!

- **Travel.** If you travel out of town on business, the cost of transportation (e.g., airfare) and lodging is fully deductible.

This is just a short list of the various tax deductions, but there are many more. Track all of your expenses so you can save some money when tax season rolls around.

## Setting Aside Funds

Nobody likes to think about giving their money away to the government. But even if you follow the tips and get some amazing tax deductions, you'll still have to pay something.

As your firm begins to grow, you will start to owe a lot in taxes. This is good, because it means you are making money and are no longer broke, but it also means you need to be prepared. Consider putting 35 percent of your profit (income minus expenses) each month into a high-interest savings account, similar to the one you opened for your firm, and make sure it is separated as money for taxes. Capital One 360's business savings account allows you to create multiple sub-accounts to separate your money. Create a sub-account for taxes and funnel all the tax money you save for the year into it. You can also have a sub-account for business savings, where you can put the general savings for your business. This will help you keep track of your tax money while still earning extra funds in interest.

And remember, PAY YOUR QUARTERLY TAXES!

### CHAPTER CHECKLIST: RUN YOUR LAW FIRM LIKE A BUSINESS

- ❒ **Create your business goals and set rewards.** Create goals for your business using the SMART framework. Set a Goal, a Stretch Goal, and a Super Stretch Goal. Set rewards for each goal.
- ❒ **Decide on a business entity and register your business.** Determine which business entity is right for your business. If necessary, speak to an accountant. Once you've settled on an entity, file all the required paperwork with your state and local governments.
- ❒ **Set up your bank accounts and credit card.** Pick a bank that works for you, and set up an operating account and an IOLTA account. Find a bank with good rates, and set up a savings account. Research credit card options and the perks and benefits of various credit cards, then select the best credit card for your business and lifestyle, and apply for the card.
- ❒ **Get malpractice insurance.** Research different malpractice insurance companies by talking to colleagues or looking at those offered through the ABA, and register for malpractice insurance.

- ❒ **Get a software for tracking your revenue and expenses.** Select an accounting software or app, register for an account, and link your bank accounts and credit card(s). Go into the software monthly to categorize revenue and expenses.
- ❒ **Get set up to pay taxes.** Register your business with the IRS (unless you are a sole proprietor or general partner). Set up a savings account just for quarterly taxes, if you will be responsible for paying them based on your business entity. Note the quarterly tax due dates on your calendar and set reminders.
- ❒ **PAY YOUR QUARTERLY TAXES!** Don't make me say it again.

CHAPTER 3

# Make Your Firm Seem Established

**OUTLINE**



Now that we've got all the business stuff taken care of, it's time to make your practice seem like an established law firm. When you're first starting out, especially broke, this part seems overwhelming. But we're going to go through it step by step, and by the end of this section of the book, you will have a professional, organized law firm.

## NAME YOURSELF

Picking a name for your firm is a big deal. You will build your entire brand around it, so select a name that reflects you and your business well.

### Naming Options

There are a few different options for choosing a name. You can select a firm name based on your own name. For example, the Law Office of Jane Doe. This is the most traditional option, but it is not helpful for marketing, and your clients don't really learn anything about you from looking at it. Plus, unless you have a really cool name, it's not very catchy.

The next option is to select a name that references your practice area, such as IP Services of Seattle. This one is good because clients will immediately know how you can serve them. And you can combine this with the name one to satisfy your ego. That's exactly what I did, when I chose Eagan Immigration.

You could also pick something that speaks to your target client, like Paternal Rights Center or Immigrant Legal Services. This is a great option from a marketing standpoint as well because it allows you to speak directly to your client and create an instant connection.

Think about the different options, the vibe you want to give off, and the clients you want to attract. You can always change the name in the future, but it's easier to get it right from the beginning.

Jot down a few different name ideas here:

1. ________________________________________
2. ________________________________________
3. ________________________________________
4. ________________________________________

Now, talk to friends and family about your ideas to get feedback. If appropriate (i.e., you aren't starting your new firm undercover while employed by another firm), post the options on social media to get an even wider response. And, if possible, talk to some target clients to get their feedback.

## Ethical Considerations

I'm throwing this in here so it's on your radar. Rule 7.1 of the ABA Model Rules of Professional Conduct prohibits a lawyer from making "a false or misleading communication about the lawyer or the lawyer's services." Model Rule 7.5 applies that general standard to firm names and letterheads. Different states interpret this differently.

Check with your state bar to ensure you comply with any ethical restrictions on naming your law firm. Some states are pretty restrictive, while others aren't, so do your homework and comply with their standards.

## Trademark

After choosing your clever name, specifically one that isn't based off your own name, you first need to make sure it's not already taken. You can check by searching the United States Patent and Trademark Office database at https://www.uspto.gov/trademarks-application-process/search-trademark-database.

If you don't find your name in there, you're probably good to go. But if your name is already taken, either pick a new name or determine whether the name is being used for a completely different business than yours. If it is, you might be in the clear.

Once you have a name, consider trademarking it to keep others from stealing it down the road. If you're a trademark attorney, then excellent, you know how to do this! But if you're not, reach out to a broke trademark attorney friend and ask for their help. Give them this book as a thank-you gift.

## GET A LOGO

Now that you've made a name for yourself (tee-hee), it's time to create a logo. Your logo is a visual representation of everything your company stands for, so think about what you want to portray. If all goes well, your logo will become the single most recognizable part of your business.

### Determining the Type of Logo You Want

There are three types of logos to choose from: typographic, illustrative, and abstract-graphic. Typographic logos have text only, such as Prada, Sony, and IBM. These logos use colors and fonts to distinguish them from normal text.

Illustrative logos literally illustrate what the company does, such as when a painting company uses a paintbrush in its logo or Red Lobster's red lobster. For a law firm, you could use the boring ole gavel or scales of justice, but I suggest you be more creative. You want to stand out to your clients.

Abstract-graphic logos, such as the Nike swoosh and the Target bull's-eye, use symbols that become linked to the company's brand. This makes you stand out, especially as you grow.

### Inspiration

When thinking about your logo, answer the following questions:

1. Who is my target market?
2. Who are my main competitors?
3. What differentiates me from my competitors?
4. What emotions and feelings do I want my logo to evoke?

It can be hard to come up with ideas for a logo, especially if you aren't particularly creative. Visit some of your favorite websites, particularly those of your competitors. When I was thinking about my logo, I visited the websites of many respectable immigration law firms to see what they had done. Even though my logo looks completely different, I got ideas on style and colors.

In addition to looking at your competitors, think about art and symbols you particularly like. Is there an image that represents the type of law you practice? Do you prefer abstract shapes? What about symbols from nature? All of these things can be incorporated into your firm's logo, and taking inspiration from things you like will help you create a logo you love.

Also consider color when designing your logo. Colors evoke certain emotions, so select colors that best represent your firm. Use the following chart to help you figure out which color best represents your brand.[1]

| Color | Emotions | Brands |
|---|---|---|
| Green | Nature<br>Calm<br>Envy<br>Good luck<br>Fresh | BP<br>John Deere<br>Spotify |
| Blue | Dependability<br>Trust<br>Stability<br>Strength | Skype<br>Oreo<br>Dell |
| Purple | Creative<br>Wise<br>Royal<br>Romantic | Yahoo!<br>Syfy<br>Hallmark Channel |
| Red | Passion<br>Youth<br>Bold<br>Powerful | Coke<br>Kmart<br>CNN |
| Orange | Optimism<br>Warm<br>Balance<br>Success | Nickelodeon<br>Harley-Davidson<br>Eagan Immigration (just throwing that in there) |
| Yellow | Clear<br>Cheerful<br>Fun<br>Friendly | Shell<br>Nikon<br>Best Buy |
| Gray | Balance<br>Quality<br>Sophistication | Apple<br>Honda<br>Swarovski |

Using this guide, I initially went with shades of blue for my logo. For my client base, dependability and trust are extremely important, and I want potential clients to feel they

[1] I really wanted to give you a fun, colorful image, but that would have cost an arm and a leg to print, and I still live the broke mind-set. So, sorry, you're just getting a lame black-and-white chart.

can trust me just by looking at my logo. But over time, as my firm developed, I realized that all the emotions orange evokes are key elements of my business, and I decided to rebrand.

Think about what is important to your clients, and find the color that corresponds to that emotion. Are you working with artists? Maybe purple is the best color for you. Do you focus on environmental law? Go green!

### Designing a Logo on a Budget

Once you come up with some inspiration and guidelines for your logo, it's time to create it. Since you're broke, you can't afford to waste hundreds of dollars on a fancy-schmancy logo from a designer. You may be able to do this in a few years and decide to revamp your logo, but not now.

Fortunately, there are lots of websites that will help you create a logo for free. Just do a quick Google search for "Free logo design," and many options will pop up. The company I used when I began my practice is Logo Garden (www.logogarden.com). Like many of its competitors, Logo Garden allows you to create a logo by selecting one of their predesigned symbols, adding text, and then customizing the color of the symbol, the font, and the text. It also allows you to play with shadowing, color fading, and some other effects. The logo options are fairly basic but well done. In fact, I later paid a small fee to another company to update my logo, and I actually preferred the logo I got from Logo Garden.

After you design your logo, download it in all the different formats the logo program offers. My favorite format is PNG file, because it basically puts your logo on a clear background. This makes the logo look very professional when uploaded on social media and websites.

## FIND OFFICE SPACE

To seem established to your potential clients, you need a professional office space where you can meet with them, receive mail, and work on their cases. When potential clients first meet with you, they should feel like you have your act together and run a respectable company that they can trust to accomplish their goals. There's no better way to give this impression than by inviting potential clients to meet with you in a nice, clean, well-decorated office.

For the broke lawyer, having such an office seems impossible. In Washington, DC, a small, one-room interior office can cost over $1,500 per month. That is outrageous! No, broke lawyer, you cannot afford such an office at this stage of the game. So what are going to do about presenting that professional feel?

### Introducing, the Virtual Office

A virtual office is one in which you and any future staff work primarily from home but rent office space only to meet with clients. This is an excellent setup for a new practice for a number of reasons.

First, operating a virtual office significantly cuts down on costs. When I first started, I found a beautiful, professional shared office space that cost me $79 per month for the mailbox and then $20 per hour for meeting rooms. Since I only met with clients for a total of about five hours per month for the first few months of my practice, this was a steal. And now that I meet with clients all the time, I have a 40-hour-per-month plan, which includes unlimited printing, copying, and scanning and allows me access to two different office locations for only $600 per month.

Second, having a virtual office allows you the flexibility to work when and where you want, and you save a lot of time on your commute. If you are focused enough that you can work from home, you can set up an office space there and work anytime, without worrying about traffic, parking, or changing out of your pajamas. If you don't have that kind of focus, head to the nearest library or coffee shop to work. You will have extreme flexibility, and clients never need to know you work from home every day.

Third, virtual offices often come with perks. My office has a spacious, comfortable cafe where I can work when I'm not renting office space. The cafe is stocked with nice mugs for coffee, tea, and hot cocoa, which I always offer my clients. On top of that, the virtual office has a secretary who greets all guests and, for an extra fee, can answer all your phone calls. The office also has a gym, which I can use whenever I want. Not only do I get an office space to use, but I also get the whole downtown office experience.

Finally, as you grow your practice, you can train your staff to work virtually as well. Although you will probably need to purchase computers and small printers for them, you will save a ton of money by not renting a larger office space or purchasing desks, chairs, and bookshelves for them. Plus, you can market the position as one that values flexibility and independence, which is a huge selling point. People are often willing to work for a lower salary in exchange for such flexibility.

## Where to Find a Virtual Office

Virtual offices are becoming more and more common, so you should be able to find something wherever you live. Type *Virtual office [name of your city]*, and many options will likely pop up. The company I use is Carr Workplaces (www.carrworkplaces.com). I now have two virtual office locations with them, and both are very well-designed and professional. Carr Workplaces has locations in 10 different states, and I have been impressed with all the locations I have visited so far. If Carr Workplaces has a location near you, check them out.

Another company that many attorneys use is Regus. Regus is larger than Carr Workplaces, and it was slightly more expensive when I was looking for a location in Washington, DC. However, Regus has offices in almost every state, which is convenient if you need to find an office space in a pinch or if you will be meeting clients in many different locations. See if you can find someone who uses a Regus near you to get real feedback.

In the last few years, a company called WeWork has popped up around the country. WeWork has a more casual work environment, with beer on tap and dogs allowed in the workplace. The decor has a hipster vibe, and the offices are usually made completely of glass. When looking into WeWork as a potential office space, think about your target market. For me, this type of space would not work because my clients are very nervous meeting a lawyer for the first time, and it's important for me to have a professional setting that puts them at ease. However, I know other attorneys who work with start-up companies and a younger crowd, and they love the WeWork style.

You can also look for virtual office space on a smaller scale. Many organizations are starting to include shared office spaces as part of their membership. Look into your local bar associations to see what they offer. One organization is Hera Hub, which assists women as they start their business. Do research online but also ask your colleagues to see what they know about virtual space. Often you'll find locations that are not heavily advertised but are more affordable and accommodating.

Another option is to make an agreement with a larger law firm or company in which you pay them a certain amount per hour or per month to use their conference room for your meetings. The only drawback to this might be branding issues, if the other law firm's name is on the door but you want to be seen as an independent entity. So think about this carefully and come up with an agreement that works for both you and the "landlord" business.

When searching for the right virtual office for you, treat the search like an interview process. Call multiple companies and locations to find out their pricing and amenities. If the initial price is too high, explain that you are just starting out and ask if they have a more basic, less expensive package. Usually, they do. Once you've narrowed it down to your top few locations, set up appointments to meet with the managers and tour the offices. Have a list of questions ready and try to view the offices from a client's perspective.

## Add Your New Address to Google Maps

Once you select an office space, add your address to Google Maps. That way, when a potential client types your firm name into their GPS, your address will pop up. This will make you look legitimate and established.

To add your address to Google Maps, go to www.google.com/maps. Type your law firm's new address into the search bar and press Enter. Once Google Maps locates the address, it will give you options on the left side of the page, below the search bar. One of the options is "Add your business." Press that button, and fill in the information. Add your law firm's name in the "Name" box.[2]

[2] Note that these instructions were accurate at the time of writing. Google changes things all the time, so if these steps aren't working for you, just google *how to add my business to Google Maps* and you should get up-to-date instructions.

After you submit your information to Google, they will mail a code to your office address with instructions on what to do next. Follow the instructions, and Google will add your name to Google Maps. Now, anytime you or anyone else enters your law firm's name on Google Maps, your address will automatically pop up.

## GET A PERSONALIZED DOMAIN NAME

If you want your business to seem established, you need a custom domain name to use for your email address and website. Follow these six tips for choosing a domain name:

1. **Keep it short and easy to type.** The longer your domain name, the more likely potential clients will misspell it. And if you use slang or shorthand (*u* instead of *you*) or words with variant spellings (*express* vs. *xpress*), it might be harder for customers to find your site. Keep it short and simple.
2. **Use keywords.** Many law firms simply use the name of their firm as their domain, but you can try using keywords to describe the type of law you practice or the services you offer. If you practice bankruptcy law, consider registering with Debt-Free.com or BankruptcyLawyer.com. You can also include your target area—for example, DenverTrademarkLawyer.com. Include the keywords that people use when searching for your services. It helps improve your rank on search engines and makes it easier for potential clients to find you.
3. **Avoid numbers and hyphens.** Using numbers and hyphens can cause confusion. When people hear your website read out loud, they don't know if you're using a numeral (3) or if it's spelled out (three). And they often misplace or forget the dash. Eliminate these from your domain name to keep it simple.
4. **Research it.** Once you've created a domain name, research it to make sure it isn't trademarked, copyrighted, or being used by another company. Use Instant Domain Search (www.instantdomainsearch.com) to quickly check domain names to determine whether yours is available. If your domain name is already taken, you can either try buying it from the current owner or come up with another domain name. Since you're broke, I recommend coming up with something new.
5. **Use an appropriate domain name extension.** Extensions are suffixes, such as .com or .net, at the end of Web addresses. These can have specific uses, such as .gov for government entities or .org for organizations, so choose one that works for your business. The .com domain extension is the most popular, and the most professional. If possible, try out multiple domain names until you find one that has .com available. If you're using the name of your firm as your domain, this might be fairly easy. But if you're using a more creative and memorable domain name, you may find it's already taken.
6. **Act fast.** Domain names sell quickly. Thankfully, they're usually inexpensive, so register your favorite domain names as soon as possible. You can register them with several different entities; google *Register a domain* to see if any of the big

companies currently have a good sale. I just performed this search and saw that GoDaddy is offering to register one domain for $0.99. If you can't find a good deal, use Google. Go to Google Domains (https://domains.google) to register your domain for $12 per year.

## SET UP YOUR FIRM EMAIL ADDRESS

Now that you have a personalized domain name, you can use it for your new email address. I recommend using Google for many aspects of your business, and email is no exception. Since many people use Gmail for their personal email, using it for business email makes for an easy transition. Once you set it up with your domain name, it will look like a personalized account to all clients and contacts. Plus, Google is inexpensive for a business account, starting at only $6 per user per month. This works well for your tight budget.

To set up a personalized email address through Google, you must set up a Google Apps for Work account. Simply google *Google Apps for Work* or go to https://apps.google.com/. Then select the "Get Started" button and follow the instructions.

On the next page, it will ask if you want to use a domain you have already purchased or buy a new domain. If you followed the steps in the previous chapter and purchased a domain name, select the button for using a domain name you already purchased and enter it in the space provided. If you haven't registered your domain name but want to do so with Google, press the other button and take this opportunity to register your new domain.

Once you have followed all the steps, Google will create a business account for you using your domain name. It will run like a normal Gmail account, although you will have some additional options that are designed only for businesses. For example, you will be able to replace the Google logo with your firm logo (I'll help you get one of those later), and you'll be able to add users as your firm grows using the Admin button. Familiarize yourself with your new account, using any tutorials necessary to better understand it.

### Link Your Email to Your Devices

You want to have access to your email at any time, from anywhere. Now that your account is set up, link it to all devices you commonly use. I have my email account linked to my cell phone, my iPad, and my Surface Pro (which is my primary work computer). Although I have set aside specific times to check my email during the day, I like to have quick access on my phone in case of a client emergency. Turning waiting into productivity saves me time later in the day.

If you link your email to multiple devices, you must protect your clients by having a good security system. Set up a password on all devices, and it doesn't hurt to require a second password to log in to the email account on each device. Also ensure your devices have programs that allow you to wipe them in case they are lost or stolen. Most phones come with this option now, so turn it on in your phone's settings. Attorney–client confidentiality is very important, and you need to protect your clients' information at all costs.

## Add a Personalized Signature

Now that your email is set up, make it even more professional by adding a personalized signature. This will display at the end of all your emails and will give clients a good impression of you as an attorney. To set up your signature, click on the settings icon in the upper right corner of your Gmail account. Then press "Settings." On the General tab, scroll down to the Signature section and press the button for a signature. Fill in your signature. It should include your name, position, and contact information. For example:

Sincerely,
**Lauren A. Eagan, Esq.**
Founder | Eagan Immigration
Tel: (202) 709-6439
www.eaganimmigration.com

*NOTICE: This e-mail message and all attachments transmitted with it are intended solely for the use of the addressee and may contain legally privileged and confidential information. If the reader of the message is not the intended recipient, or an employee or agent responsible for delivering the message to the intended recipient, you are hereby notified that any dissemination, distribution, copying, or other use of the message or its attachments is strictly prohibited. If you have received a message in error, please notify the sender immediately by replying to the message and please delete it from your computer.*
***Please consider the environment before printing this email.***

When I first started my practice, I also included my address below my name. However, I now have multiple addresses and that got too wordy. Also notice that I have included buttons that link to my social media. I will teach you how to create those when we get to the social media chapter, but until then, create your signature without them.

If you plan to use your phone to access your email, you will also want to set up a personalized signature there. Once you have linked your email account to your phone, log in, select Settings, and select the account. Add a signature in the signature section. The signature I use for emails from my phone is:

Sincerely,
Lauren A. Eagan, Esq.
Eagan Immigration

Tel: (202) 709-6439
www.eaganimmigration.com
*Email sent from my phone—please excuse any typos

Note the last line, in which I alert the recipient that I am sending from my phone and apologize for any typos. This is important, because although typos look unprofessional, people are more forgiving when you acknowledge, explain, and apologize.

## GET AN OFFICE PHONE LINE

When you start your own firm, do not hand out your cell phone number for clients to call you. To seem established, you need a separate business line.

### Virtual Office Secretary

If you have chosen a virtual office space, the company may offer a secretary to assist with answering phones. If this is included, great, but usually it is an additional cost. And since you're broke, we want to keep the additional costs to a minimum. However, if the secretary is affordable, move forward with follow-up questions. What does the secretary say when answering the phone? Can you provide a script for them to follow? Does the secretary transfer calls to you or just take messages? Think of additional questions that are relevant to your business and ask them.

Often, the secretaries at virtual office spaces are working for many different companies, so they are limited in the amount they can personalize their calls. Since you are just starting your firm, it is important that the secretary reflect the image you want to portray of your business. This person may be the first contact the potential client has with your firm.

### Google Voice

Google Voice is an excellent option to your phone. It is a phone number that routes through a phone you already own, such as your cell phone. It allows you to set up a voice mail specifically for the Google Voice number, make calls directly from your cell phone using the Google Voice number, and send text messages from the Google Voice number. It also transcribes your voice mails, gives you the option to forward them to your email, and allows you to set times for your phone to ring from the Google Voice number.

There are quite a few benefits to Google Voice, and I'll go through them in order of importance. First and foremost, it's free! You can't beat that when you're broke.

Google Voice also allows you to select a phone number with the area code you want. This is important, because it makes it seem like the number routes to an office line, rather than a cell phone. Having an area code from the city in which your office is located makes you seem legitimate. You can use this phone number for both incoming and outgoing calls and can set your phone to ask you which number to use every time you make a call.

With your Google Voice account, you can set up a personalized voice mail greeting that callers will hear if you don't answer the phone. Even though you may use the same phone for your personal line and your business line, callers will only hear the voice mail greeting that corresponds to the phone number they called. This means that your potential clients will hear, "You have reached the Law Office of . . ." not, "What's up?! Chris here. You know what to do." Remember, we're striving for professionalism.

Those are just a few of the benefits of Google Voice. There are many others, such as the ability to text and transcribe, and its portability, but I will leave you to explore a little yourself.

As your practice grows, you may find that Google Voice no longer works for you. Fortunately, you can easily transfer the phone number to another company, which makes Google Voice an excellent, free option as you're getting your firm off the ground.

## GET A FAX NUMBER

Okay, I realize that faxes were cool in the '80s and nobody really uses them anymore. In the age of email, fax seems ridiculous and outdated. However, I use my business fax at least once a month. Government entities still use fax pretty consistently, and I have many low-literacy clients who aren't email savvy but who know how to get to the nearest Kinko's and fax me documents. So, here are some tips on getting fax for your firm.

### Use Your Virtual Office's Fax

Before you try to set something up for yourself, find out if your virtual office offers a fax service. If it's free or really cheap, go with that one. It will take the hassle out of finding another service, and the virtual office company will probably put the faxes straight into your mailbox. The only downside is that you will need to be in the office to send or receive a fax. If you only plan to be in the office a couple days per week, this might not be the best fit.

### HelloFax

If you went with Google Voice, I have another fabulous Google product for you. It's called HelloFax. This allows you to send faxes online, no paper or scanning required. Just upload the document you want to send into HelloFax and input the fax number of the recipient. HelloFax will then send the fax online to the receiving fax machine. No need to print, scan, prepare a cover sheet, and so on. HelloFax does everything for you.

On the receiving end, HelloFax will give you a fax number in the area code you select, and you can treat this number as a normal fax machine number. When clients send you documents by fax, they will use your fax number, and anything they send will come into HelloFax as a pdf. HelloFax will also forward the incoming fax to your email so you get it right away. It makes the process pretty painless.

HelloFax is inexpensive compared to other online fax services, but their least expensive plan costs $99 per year. This is a lot when you're broke. I recommend selecting a fax company you want to use but waiting until you actually need to fax something or a client needs to fax something to you before officially setting up your number and paying the fee. This way, you can spread out your start-up costs so you don't spend more than you earn. If you want a fax number you can put on your business cards, see if the fax company you selected has a free, limited plan. HelloFax does. It's pretty limited, only allowing five free fax pages a month, but at least you will get a fax number, and you can simply upgrade when it becomes necessary.

## DESIGN AND LAUNCH A WEBSITE

Designing a website is a huge undertaking, but it is vital to the growth of your business. Nowadays, people spend more time online than in the real world, so having a solid website is the key to making your firm seem established. In this section, I will talk about different website hosting platforms I recommend, what you should include on your website, and options for designing your website on a budget.

### Website Hosting

Having a good website is extremely important. I did a lot of research on different website hosting platforms, and I ultimately went with Wix. I will tell you a little more about Wix in a minute, but I want to encourage you to do your own research on this topic. Every year, newer, better platforms come to market, and it's important to read the most recent reviews and compare prices. I will tell you what I did initially and what I've learned since.

#### *Wix*

When I first built my website, I shopped around to a few different platforms, and in the end I went with Wix. I like Wix because it is user-friendly. I can easily update my website myself, without requesting help from a professional. I also think it looks nice and has a lot of good extras that make the website look professional and interactive. However, Wix does not support a bilingual website, so I had to design two separate websites, and link them to each other using "English" and "Español" buttons. That was a decent fix, but not ideal for me.

A huge benefit of Wix, however, is the price. You can start out with a website for FREE. That's a big deal, especially since you're broke. The downside of the website being free is that Wix will post its logo on your website as a form of advertising. So essentially you are trading advertising for a website. You can upgrade to a premium plan to get rid of the Wix logo, and premium plans run from $6.50 to $25 per month. However, Wix often runs good promotions on their annual subscriptions, which dramatically reduces the price.

When I built my website, I started with the free version with the logo, waited until I earned a little money in my practice, and purchased the premium plan during a good sale. They have sales all the time. Take your time before purchasing the premium plan so you can get a good deal.

### WordPress

A few years after starting my firm, I went through the whole rebranding process, including updating my website. This time around, I hired a professional who moved away from Wix and switch to WordPress. Since then, I have used WordPress for projects outside the firm, and I think it's a great option for a first website.

WordPress has been around for quite a while, so there are many tutorials for using it. It also has more programs that integrate with it, which means you can add cooler features (like multiple languages) to your site.

When I first started using WordPress, I found it a little harder to use than Wix in terms of the actual site creation and design. Wix is extremely visual, so you can manipulate things easily and see exactly how the changes will look. With WordPress, you have to jump through more hoops, especially with visual changes. This is challenging at first, but you'll get the hang of it.

WordPress, like Wix, also has a free option. It will, of course, include advertisements, but it's a good option to get you up and running. Once you start bringing in clients, you can start paying a subscription and get the ads removed.

## What Should You Have on Your Website?

Now that you've picked out a host for your website, you actually need to fill it with content. I will give you an outline of the different sections your website should include, but you can also visit my website (www.eaganimmigration.com) or other respectable firms' websites for ideas. When I first started designing my website, I found my top five favorite law firm websites and basically pulled ideas to create my own. Don't reinvent the wheel.

Please note that every page should have a header and a footer. At a minimum, the header should contain your firm name, and the footer should contain your contact information.

### The Home Page

Your home page needs to draw the potential client in. It should look professional yet interesting, such as with eye-catching photos—either photos of attorneys working with clients, scenery from the area where the firm is located, or art that is relevant to the practice area. These photos always draw me in and make we want to learn more about the law firm. I also recently noticed firms adding videos to the home page in place of photos. This is a new trend that helps draw potential clients in.

Include a summary of your firm and your mission. You should have outlined this in your business plan, and your website is the place to portray your mission to your clients. You can elaborate on it in the "About the Firm" section but put something on the home page to give potential clients a sense of who you are.

Many firms include recent news and updates on the home page. This creates even more visual interest and shows potential clients that the website is active. Update this section at least once a week. Not only does it show clients your website has the latest information, but it will also help boost your ratings in Web searches.

### *About*

In this section, you tell potential clients more about yourself and your firm. On my website, I found it easiest to divide the "About" section into subsections. I have a page for my firm overall and a page for me and my staff.

Use the Our Firm tab to cover your mission and how you will help your clients. This does not need to be a long section, but you should make the potential client feel like you are there to help them. This is where you should really try and connect with the potential client and his or her needs.

On the page dedicated to you, talk about your experience and your interests. Think about your target market, and try to write about yourself in a way that they would find appealing. Are your typical clients very family oriented? Include some personal details about your own family. Are they tech-savvy? Highlight ways in which you use tech to streamline your firm.

### *Practice Areas*

This section is the most tedious but one of the most important. I have had many clients tell me that they want to hire me for XYZ, and they know I do this type of work because I talked about it on my website.

The practice areas section is also important because you will fill it up with keywords that will help people find your website through Web searches. For example, if a potential client googles *lawyer asylum*, my website would not pop up based on the home page alone. But it will pop up because I have a whole practice area page dedicated to asylum.

Figuring out how to break down your practice areas can be tricky; look at websites of similar law firms to get examples. When I prepared my website, I looked at the websites of other immigration law firms that I knew had a humanitarian focus. This gave me some ideas for how to present my expertise to my clients in a coherent, logical manner.

### *Testimonials*

The Testimonial page adds a humanizing element to your website. This is especially important if you work mainly with individuals as opposed to businesses. Individuals want to see that you are successful and will do a good job for them. This is why companies like Yelp are so popular. People want to know they are getting the best service, based on the reviews of others.

If you worked at a law firm prior to opening your own practice, ask your former clients to write reviews that you can put on your website. If you explain you are opening your own firm, many former clients will be happy to help. If you've never worked at a law firm before but have some legal experience (e.g., handled cases pro bono or worked in a legal clinic), the clients you worked with may also be willing to give you a testimonial.

In addition to client testimonials, you can get testimonials from colleagues. Ask your contacts from law school or former legal positions to write a testimonial for your website. Ask them to focus on qualities that will make you appealing to your clients, such as your drive, compassion, and honesty.

When posting these testimonials on your website, keep in mind ethical considerations and maintain attorney–client privilege. Ask the client's permission. And don't use last names or other identifying information. I often post the testimonial with a photo of the client, but if the case is especially sensitive, I usually post a stock photo and only use the client's initials. You will need to use your best judgment and put your clients first when designing your testimonials page.

### Resources

I suggest creating a Resources page for a couple of reasons. First, it makes you look like a nice, helpful attorney who wants people to succeed, whether or not they are clients. Second, it is a good place to put resources you use often, so you can find them quickly when you need them. You can also point current clients to the Resources page when they have questions that can be answered there. For example, when a client wants to know how long they have to wait for their visa to process, I direct them to a website on my Resources page that will tell them the status of their case. This is helpful to the client, cuts down on work for me, and directs clients to my website, which helps boost Web traffic and search ratings.

If you work in multiple practice areas, you can create a few subpages with different links pertaining to the practice area. I suggest giving a one-line description prior to the link, so people know what it is for. In addition to links, you can also add news articles, reports, or informational videos that are relevant to the type of law you practice. I have my Resources page broken down into subpages, which include a few different practice areas, a News & Publications page, and an Informational Videos page.

### Contact

A Contact page is a must, and should be easy to find on your website. You want to make it as easy as possible for potential clients to reach you. Provide your phone number and email address, and add a contact form that potential clients can fill out to request information about their case. The contact form should request the potential client's name, email address, phone number, and a message. That way, when you receive the message from the contact form, you will have the potential client's information for follow-up.

On my website, I have the addresses to both of my offices, along with maps to create some visual stimulation. I have included an email address that goes to a more generic account, info@eaganimmigration.com, and not my personal account. I want to protect my personal account from the crazies and spam. My telephone number is prominently displayed, to make it easy for potential clients to spot it on the page. I also have a contact form that automatically forwards responses to my email. The goal of the Contact page is to drive potential clients to your business.

These six pages will give you a complete, useful, and interesting website that will show potential clients you are established. More than anything, potential clients fear their attorney will abandon or take advantage of them, and having a robust website creates a sense of stability and professionalism.

## How to Design a Website on a Budget

The most challenging part of creating a website is designing it. The content takes a long time to prepare, but as an attorney, you should be used to writing. The hard part is figuring out how to add pages, insert media, select appropriate colors and fonts, and organize everything in a professional manner. There are individuals who dedicate their entire careers to Web design, but frankly, you can't afford them right now. Fortunately, you have a few other options.

### *DIY*

The first option is to do it yourself. A huge benefit to this is that you learn a lot throughout the process, and you won't have to depend on anyone to make updates to your website in the future. Plus, you save a ton of money.

If you're going to do it yourself, find about five professional websites you love and use them as a guide. Make a list of the things you like about each website. Is it the color palette? The font style? How do they employ visual stimulation and media? Create a list for each of the websites you've selected, and then figure out what they have in common. You want to create a website that is different from your samples, but you can use your favorite features to guide your design.

Use the tutorials from the web hosting service you selected to learn how the features work. Really pay attention, and take notes. Most Web hosts have templates that you can use as a base and modify; find one that works well with your list of favorite website features. Use this template as a starting point for your website.

Before adding any content to your website, create a separate document that simply outlines the pages and subpages you want to include. Decide what to include on each page and whether you will need any special features, such as photos, videos, or lists.

Once you have a solid outline, start designing your website, referring to the tutorials as necessary. Remember, you want to include your firm name and logo on every page in the header. You will also include your contact information in the footer. Add this first. Then start building out the pages. Don't add content yet, but simply add and name each page, so you have a base. When all your pages are laid out, format them, putting in the right backgrounds and colors on each page.

Now that you have a base, start adding the content. This will probably take a long time, because you want to make sure the fonts are consistent, everything lines up correctly, and it is easy to read or view. Not to mention coming up with the content itself. Expect the Web design portion of starting your firm to take many, many hours, but it is worth it. Many attorneys put off designing a website, and I believe that detracts from their credibility. You may be broke, but you're smart, and your website will help propel your business forward.

### Get Help from a Web-Design Friend

Many young Web designers are trying to build a portfolio, and often they will help friends design websites in order to do this. If you don't have any Web-design friends, ask around to see if anyone else has a friend looking to build up their portfolio. You'd be surprised how many people know somebody with Web-design experience. If you do not feel comfortable taking the services for free, see if the designer will barter with you. Can you provide him or her legal services in exchange for the design?

Even if you find someone who can design your website, you will still be responsible for preparing the content. When I built my website, I combined help from a friend (my husband) with the do-it-yourself approach. My husband is an engineer and is familiar with computer programming, but he had never designed a website before. We worked together on the project, selecting the style and format together and discussing different options for page layout and media. Then my husband created all the pages, making sure everything was formatted properly, and I filled in the content. We both spent many hours on the project, but it was nice to have a companion. If you have a close friend or family member who is willing to help but doesn't have Web-design experience, take advantage of their offer and put their other skills to good use.

### Buy an Existing Website

Do you know any attorneys who are going out of business? Perhaps they are retiring or moving to a larger firm. If the attorney currently has a good website, consider offering to buy it. You are broke, so think of something you can reasonably afford. It's likely the attorney has not even considered selling their website and will jump at the chance to make a little extra cash. But if you can't come to an agreement that works with your budget, don't make the purchase.

If you purchase an existing website, you still need to redo a lot of the content. Be prepared to invest a lot of time on this, but know you will save time on design and formatting.

## GET A PROFESSIONAL HEADSHOT

When you start your own firm, you absolutely must have a professional photo to use on your website, in your email, and on social media. If you already have a professional photo from a prior job, use that one and save your money. If you don't, get one before or shortly after starting your firm.

### How to Get a Headshot Cheap

One of the best ways to get a professional photo is to have a friend or contact with photography experience take it for you. Many young photographers are trying to build their portfolios and are often comfortable taking a simple headshot for free or very cheap. Using this method, I got my first few professional headshots done for free. The first time I got one taken, the photographer owed my boss a favor and did the headshots for our entire firm. This was prior to starting my own firm. The second time, the photographer was a member of a networking group I was part of and offered free headshots to other members. On both occasions, I got professional headshots for free. Start thinking about who you know with photography experience, and reach out to them. They may be willing to cut you a deal or even take your headshot for free.

If you can't find a personal contact to take your headshot, ask your colleagues for suggestions and do some online research. If your colleagues don't have recommendations, look for photographers on Yelp. Since saving money is paramount, shop around for the best deal. You should be able to find a pretty reasonable price on a headshot with some work.

### What to Wear

Dress professionally for your headshot. Most attorneys wear a dark-colored suit, either black, dark gray, or navy blue. Pair that with a nice blouse for women and a collared shirt and tie for men. Select shirts with color, and stay away from white or beige, as it can wash you out. Also avoid crazy prints, as they are distracting. You want you viewers to focus on you, not your fun shirt.

If your firm and clientele are very casual, you may choose to dress in a business-casual style for your headshot. For ladies, I recommend a nice blouse or sweater with pants, or a professional dress. For men, slacks and a polo or sweater.

Remember, even if you are extremely casual and so are your clients, most clients want to know their attorney can at least clean up for a photo and that you know how to get it together and advocate on their behalf.

## SET UP SOCIAL MEDIA ACCOUNTS FOR YOUR FIRM

Social media is a very important part of business marketing these days. At the inception of your firm, set up social media accounts on many different platforms, such as Facebook, LinkedIn, Instagram, Twitter, and any other platform relevant to the type of law you practice. Make sure to add as much information as you can about your business, and include your headshot or logo as the main photos on each platform.

Once you have created your social media accounts, keep them active so they start to look established. To save time posting across multiple platforms, open an account with Hootsuite (www.hootsuite.com). You can connect up to three social media accounts to your Hootsuite account for free. If you upgrade to a premium Hootsuite account, you can add additional accounts. After you link your accounts to Hootsuite, create your post in Hootsuite, and it will post to all linked social media accounts. This saves a ton of time.

To remain active, set up a schedule for posting to social media. When I first started my practice, I posted to social media every Monday, Wednesday, and Friday at 10:00 a.m. Having this set time helped me keep on track, and after a few weeks, my social media pages started to look more robust and established.

## ORDER BUSINESS CARDS

Now that you have an address, phone number, email address, and website, it's time to order business cards. Search different companies online to order your business cards and compare prices. Vistaprint usually has great deals, which helps when starting a firm on a budget.

Now it's time to design your business card. Since you're on a budget, make sure you conform to the restrictions that will get you the best price. For example, you might only be able to order one-sided business cards. You may also have to get the most basic finish. At the inception of your law firm, these minor downgrades are just fine, and it's unlikely any potential client or contact will notice. Once your firm takes off and you're rolling in cash, you can upgrade to the flashier business card you've always dreamed of.

When designing your business card, keep your logo in mind. You may not be able to include the actual logo on your business card, depending on its style, price restrictions, and the overall look you're going for. However, select fonts and colors that complement your logo whether or not it's included. You want to create a cohesive look in every element of your firm.

## SET UP CREDIT CARD PAYMENTS

Accepting credit card payments can seem scary to the broke lawyer because of the processing fees. We think, *But if I charge $10,000 and 2.9 percent of that goes to the credit card company, I lose $290 of that!* Yes, but you keep $9,710, which you might not have otherwise received if you didn't accept credit cards. Accepting credit cards makes it so easy for clients to pay, even if they don't have the cold, hard cash necessary for your legal fees. And if we want to make anything easy for clients, it's their ability to pay.

There are many different credit card processing companies, all with positives and negatives. Some of the most popular companies include PayPal and Stripe. PayPal is nice because its rates are reasonable, it is well-known and familiar to clients, and it will easily integrate into your website. Compare rates and look at your needs before making the best decision for your firm.

If you plan to accept trust funds by credit card, LawPay is an excellent option. In most jurisdictions, it is an ethical violation to accept trust funds by credit card because of the processing fees that are automatically deducted from the funds. However, LawPay came up with a solution for that problem. They make sure all credit card payments are fully deposited into your IOLTA account, without taking any processing fees. Instead, they deduct the processing fees from your operating account, which keeps the receipt of trust funds by credit card fully compliant with ethical guidelines.

## CHAPTER CHECKLIST: GET LEGIT

- ❒ **Select a name.** Pick a few potential options for your firm's name, and run them by friends, family, and colleagues to get their opinions. Use the feedback you receive to pick a name for your firm. Check with your state bar rules to ensure your name is compliant. Also check with the trademark office to make sure your name isn't already taken.
- ❒ **Create a logo.** Determine the style of logo you want, think about your target audience, and look at different color palettes to get started. Then design your logo using one of the inexpensive logo companies online.
- ❒ **Get office space.** Research virtual office locations near you, and select one with a plan that meets your needs. Sign up. Add your new office address to Google Maps.
- ❒ **Get a domain name.** Create a domain name personalized to you or your firm. Do some quick research to make sure it's available. Purchase the domain name online—try to find a company having a sale.
- ❒ **Set up your firm email.** Select an email hosting platform, such as Google/Gmail. Using your new domain name, set up an email account on your chosen platform. Link your email to all your devices, such as your phone and tablet. Create a personalized email signature on each device.
- ❒ **Get a phone line.** Find out if your virtual office offers an answering service, and, if so, whether it's within your budget. Or, set up Google Voice on your cell phone.
- ❒ **Get a firm fax number.** Use your virtual office's fax, if they have one. Or set up an account on HelloFax.com or another low-cost online fax service.

- ❒ **Create a website.** Select a Web-hosting platform. Outline the tabs and content of your website. Create the website yourself or with the help of a friend or family member. Or, buy an existing website.
- ❒ **Get a professional headshot.** Find a friend or family member who is good at photography and photo editing, and ask for help. Select a neutral background. Wear a professional outfit.
- ❒ **Set up social media accounts.** Create accounts on platforms relevant to your target market. Don't waste time on platforms your audience doesn't even use.
- ❒ **Order business cards.** Start with something inexpensive and basic, and try to find a sale.
- ❒ **Accept credit cards.** Select a credit card processing company. PayPal is an easy option, and LawPay is great if you will accept trust payments.

CHAPTER 4

# Getting Clients

**OUTLINE**



This is the fun (and sometimes scary) part: getting clients. Before we even delve into tips for how to get clients, you need to establish your target market. Often, new firm owners want to cast a wide net and take anything that walks in the door. While that may seem like a good idea in the short term, it can have very negative effects on your business. Instead, narrow your market and target a specific group of potential clients, which is extremely effective and is sustainable in the long-term.

## ESTABLISHING YOUR TARGET MARKET

Really understanding your target market is the most crucial element for the growth of your law firm. Specifying a target market will help you focus your marketing efforts and attract the kind of clients you want.

As you start thinking about your target market, first decide whether you want to cater to individuals or businesses. Then use the corresponding Ideal Client Worksheet to refine your ideal client even further.

### IDEAL CLIENT WORKSHEET FOR INDIVIDUALS

Before you start filling this out, take a moment to visualize your perfect client. What kind of case do they have? How old are they? What are their hobbies? Really think about it before you dive into the following questions. I even want you to pick a name.

| Name: | Age: |
|---|---|
| Gender: | Marital status: |
| Number of kids: | Ages of kids: |
| Income: | Assets: |
| Education level: | Occupation: |
| Ethnicity: | Nationality: |
| Personal goals: | Career goals: |
| Interests and hobbies: | Social media platforms: |

## IDEAL CLIENT WORKSHEET FOR BUSINESSES

Targeting businesses is a little different than targeting individuals, but remember that you ultimately have to appeal to the individuals working at the businesses. Fill out the Ideal Client Worksheet for Businesses first, and then use the Ideal Client Worksheet for Individuals to target the decision-makers in the businesses you want to serve.

| Name: | Location: |
|---|---|
| Industry: | Sector: |
| Annual revenue: | Ownership structure: |
| Number of employees: | Number of locations: |
| Year established: | Business goals: |
| Events company hosts: | Events employees attend: |
| Social media platforms: | Additional information: |

If you have more than one target market, copy the relevant Ideal Client Worksheet and fill it out for each target market. You can prepare a marketing plan for each group separately.

Although you can market to multiple target clients, consider picking just one or two. When you have a narrow focus, you can really tailor your content and target your marketing to connect deeply with that audience. It may seem counterintuitive, but many of the most successful attorneys got that way by focusing on a specific niche and a narrow target market.

Using the Ideal Client Worksheet you just filled out, write one to two sentences summarizing your target client:

____________________________________________________________

____________________________________________________________

____________________________________________________________.

Excellent. Now keep this in mind as you plan your marketing strategy and determine the best ways to find your clients.

# NETWORKING

Networking is one of the best ways to grow your practice. The most important thing to remember is that people like to give business to people they know and trust. If you want to be that person, you need to get out, meet people, and then see them over and over again until they know you well enough to trust you and send you business.

## Overcoming the Fear of Networking

If you're one of the many people who are afraid to network, use the mantra I tell myself every time I'm overwhelmed in a networking situation: "Fake it till you make it." Obviously, this phrase has many other applications in life, but in networking situations I use it to remind myself to act like everyone I'm meeting is a good friend.

Another tip is to go to the networking event armed with a few questions you can ask people as conversation starters. Think about the type of people who will be at the event, and tailor your questions accordingly. What do they do for a living? What is their age bracket? Is it a political crowd? If all else fails, find something you know they will relate to, such as, "Oh my gah, this shrimp is amazing! Who is catering this event?!" The goal is just to find a friendly way to get the conversation started.

If you're especially nervous, bring a friend in a different field. Once you get there, branch off from your friend, but having them there will give you some peace of mind knowing that you at least know someone at the event.

## Where to Network

Sometimes the hardest part about networking is deciding when and where to network. Networking can be time-consuming, so make sure the event is valuable to you and the growth of your business. As you start attending events, be strategic about it, and select events that will really grow your network of colleagues and potential clients.

### *Determine the Value of a Networking Event*

Since you're broke, you will want to start with networking events that are free or low-cost. If the event is not free, the potential value of the networking opportunity needs to justify the cost, so always think carefully before paying for a networking event.

When determining the value of a networking event, ask yourself three questions:

1. Will potential clients likely be at the networking event? Use your work on the Ideal Client Worksheet to help answer this question.

2. Will professionals with a similar target market as mine be at this networking event? Even if no potential clients will be at the event, meeting other professionals with a similar client base can be just as valuable. These are the people who, once they know and trust you, will refer potential clients to you.
3. Will I learn something at this event? Even if you will not likely get any clients from a networking event, learning something that can help you in your practice—either on the business side of things or in your legal work—is extremely valuable.

If you are unable to answer yes to any of these questions when deciding whether to attend a networking event, the value of the event to you is likely pretty low. If the event is free and you have extra time on your hands, attend it just to get your name out there. But if there is a fee to attend or you have other potential commitments, don't waste your time.

### *Finding Networking Events*

Depending on where you live, the number of networking events available to you will vary greatly. I used to practice in San Diego, California, which is a fairly laid-back city. Instead of networking, most people left work and headed to the beach. Now that I live in Washington, DC, networking is as normal as eating and sleeping. But no matter where you live, you can find or create networking events to help your practice. Even something as small as a one-on-one coffee meeting can work, as long as you do it strategically.

When looking for networking events, find legal organizations near you that focus on your specific practice area. Networking events offered by these organizations fall into the second category previously listed, catering to professionals with a similar client base as you. Sometimes it feels like attending events with this narrow a focus can be counterintuitive. What bankruptcy attorney would send a bankruptcy client to another bankruptcy attorney? That just seems bad for business. However, attorneys often send away clients for a number of reasons, such as conflicts of interest, no availability to take new cases, or specific issues the attorney does not deal with. You want to be the first person the attorney thinks of when referring the business out.

Another option is to join groups targeted at solo or small practices. These groups are great, because the attorneys meet for the express purpose of getting to know each other to ultimately refer business. Often, the meetings center around an educational presentation aimed at helping small practices. I suggest you start by reaching out to your state bar to see if they have any groups they recommend.

Next, check out alumni events through your law school or undergraduate university. Alumni tend to stick together, so if you routinely attend alumni events and get to know the regulars, they will likely start to refer business to you. Be sure to talk about what you do at these events, rather than simply rehashing the good ole days. If people don't know what you do, they can't refer business to you. Also, make sure these events fall into one of the three categories previously listed. I enjoy going to my alumni events because they're fun, but I rarely meet clients, people with the same client base, or learn anything, so I attend these events only when I don't have something better.

Finally, look for organizations that specifically target your client base and attend their networking events. For example, if you are a real estate attorney, join a local real estate association. Or if you're an immigration attorney, find a foreign professionals networking group.

When you first start your practice, attend as many networking events as possible. At each networking event, pay attention to whether the event meets one of the three prongs of a good networking event. If it does, start attending networking events with that organization regularly. If not, cross that one off your list to free up time for more fruitful events. After about six months to a year, you will really get a good idea of which events are the most valuable to you, and you can focus your time on those.

## VOLUNTEERING

Another great way to get your name out there and get new business is by volunteering. I know it seems counterproductive, because how are you going to make money by giving your services away for free? With volunteer-based marketing, your focus is long-term. By volunteering, you will build up a good reputation in the community, community representatives and potential clients will get to know you, and individuals who do not qualify for pro bono services or who need more specialized representation will end up hiring you.

There are two main ways to do volunteer-based marketing: (1) take cases on a pro bono basis and (2) volunteer at legal clinics and community events.

### Taking Pro Bono Cases

Taking pro bono cases is a great way to meet clients and spread your name throughout your target market. When you take a pro bono case, you will work one-on-one with your client, and your client will get to know you and your work product. If you work hard for your clients and show them that they can trust you as an attorney, they will ultimately end up referring you to their friends and family members with similar cases.

When taking pro bono cases, be strategic about it. Is there a particular community you want to tap into? What about a specific type of case? Be sure the pro bono cases you take are the kind of cases you want in your practice.

Finally, take pro bono cases that have been screened through a nonprofit organization. This not only ensures that you are helping a client who truly needs the assistance, but it also creates connections within the nonprofit organization. If you work with them regularly, they may begin to refer paying cases to you that they cannot take.

### Volunteering at Legal Clinics

When I first started my practice, I volunteered at three different nonprofit organizations on a weekly basis. On Thursday mornings, I would volunteer doing immigrant intakes at Catholic charities. On Friday afternoons, I would drive to the University of Maryland in Baltimore to help with their legal clinic. And on Saturday mornings, I volunteered at a general legal clinic at a church down the street. These volunteer opportunities allowed me to keep up on my legal skills, and they helped me get to know other prominent attorneys in the area. The only organization in which I am still actively involved is the legal clinic down the street, but I still get referrals from all three organizations.

As you are just starting out and have time on your hands, consider regularly volunteering at a few different legal clinics that target your preferred client base. With time, you will figure out which legal clinics have the highest value to you, and you can start narrowing it down to the top one or two that yield the most business.

The most important thing with volunteering at legal clinics is to be consistent. Find a weekly clinic and go every week. You will get to know the other volunteers and staff at the legal clinic well, and eventually they will trust you enough to send you business. It will also allow you to see some of the same clients multiple times, and soon they will start sending their friends to the clinic just to talk to you. At the legal clinic where I still volunteer, I regularly meet individuals who came to the clinic just to meet me after being referred by a friend.

Volunteering at a legal clinic is an opportunity to be the attorney clients choose to hire if they do qualify for free services through the clinic. If clients already met you at the clinic, chances are they will think of you first in the event they need to hire paid counsel. However, it is important to remain ethical and be honest with the clients. At the clinic where I volunteer, I always explain the parameters of our clinic and who we can and cannot help. If we cannot assist a particular client, I give them a referral sheet with a list of larger nonprofit organizations who may be able to help. I also give them my business card and explain that I am a for-profit attorney and charge for my services, but I tell them I would love to meet with them in my office if they decide to hire a for-profit attorney. Going through these steps ensures that clients have multiple options available to them and that I am completely up front about potential fees. Despite all this, many of the clients I meet at the legal clinic ultimately end up hiring me to represent them.

## SPEAKING AND WRITING

Speaking and writing about your practice area are great ways to build your reputation and get your name out in the community. This form of marketing is aimed at other professionals and builds your credibility. Ultimately, the goal is for other professionals to think of you first as an expert in your field when they need to refer business.

### Speaking Engagements

To get speaking engagements, first get involved in local (or national) organizations that either focus on your practice area or have members with a similar client base as you do.

Refer to the "Networking" section earlier in this chapter for more tips on how to get involved in these groups and establish relationships with the members.

Once you have established a good reputation in the group, start talking to the higher-ups about the possibility of speaking. Does the group hold an annual conference? Ask about speaking, and suggest specific topics that are your specialty areas or areas where you want to grow your practice. Does the group put on webinars? Offer to host or cohost a webinar, and again, suggest a topic. Make the process as painless as possible for the organizer of the speaking engagement by suggesting topics, being flexible with your time, and coming to the event prepared.

If you are nervous to speak in front of a crowd, consider starting with a webinar and then work your way up to in-person speaking. You can also try recording YouTube videos for your firm, so you can get in the habit of speaking and simultaneously create marketing content for your firm.

## Writing

Writing not only spreads knowledge in the legal community, but having a list of publications also looks great on your website and curriculum vitae. The more publications you have, the more credible and experienced you appear. You can either write articles that your target client will read or articles that your colleagues and potential referral partners will read. Before you even start writing, think about the audience and prepare your written work accordingly.

There are two great ways to target potential clients through your writing. The first is by creating a blog that links to your website and regularly publishing articles on that platform. The second way to target clients is to write for a large legal publishing company. As I discussed earlier in the book, when I first started my practice I published a number of articles on Nolo.com. I made a little money publishing these articles, and I boosted my credibility as an attorney by adding to my list of publications.

When writing articles that target the client, limit the use of legalese. Try talking like a regular person, and explain things as clearly as possible. Also, consider your target clientele. Are they well educated? Do they have a specific profession? Do they speak another language? Ask yourself these questions and more to determine exactly what your target client is most likely to read, and then incorporate your findings into your writing. Use keywords, and think of a title that is catchy and will draw your target client to you.

On the other hand, when writing for publications aimed at other attorneys or high-level professionals, adjust your writing style accordingly. In these publications, you will likely cite cases and resources you used. You will analyze legal decisions or make predictions on upcoming legislation. If you are using the article as a platform to explain the law to other attorneys, you can do so in a much more complex fashion.

Again, think about your target audience and what they want to read. Prepare your writing accordingly.

## SOCIAL MEDIA

I could go on and on about how awesome social media has been for my business. And don't worry, I will later. But before I do that, look back at the Ideal Client Worksheet to remind yourself what type of social media will best reach your ideal client. Even though you can have all sorts of social media accounts, you should focus on that one.

In addition to what you will learn in this chapter, there are many books on marketing using social media that go into all the different strategies in greater detail. My favorite one so far is *One Million Followers—How I Built a Massive Social Following in 30 Days* by Brendan Kane. This book gives a good overview of the different social media platforms while also giving specific tips to help grow your following.

Before you even delve into all the other books out there, start here for a solid, law-focused overview of marketing using social media.

### Facebook

At the time of this writing, 2.4 billion people had Facebook accounts. That is a huge potential market, and you should take advantage of this for your business. We already talked about creating a Facebook page for your business, but this section provides the strategies on turning that Facebook page into a huge business generator.

First, get as many people as possible to follow your Facebook page. Start with friends and family, just to get enough followers to make your page look legit. Then ask your existing and past clients (if you have any) to follow you on Facebook. When you have a consultation, mention your Facebook page, and suggest the potential client follow it. When you're broke and in the beginning stages of starting your firm, these are the best first steps for getting your Facebook page going.

Once you have a little extra revenue to spend on marketing, start using Facebook ads. You can set the monetary limit you want to spend on advertising each month when creating the ad, and Facebook will not go over that limit. My limit is $150 per month, and I usually end up spending between $120 and $150. When creating your ad, refer back to your Ideal Client Worksheet. Create the ad based on your ideal client's location, age, gender, language, and any interests. Select the images you want to display in your ad and any text. Keep it simple.

Here's a sample Facebook ad that I use for my business: My ad is targeted at male and female Spanish speakers from Central America who live within 100 miles of either my Washington, DC, office or my McLean, Virginia, office, and are between 18 and 55 years old. I also added "futbol" as an interest, because about 99.9 percent (rough, but probably very accurate estimate) of people from Central America love soccer. My ad has my Facebook page's cover photo and says, "Did you come to the United States fleeing threats in your country? Follow us to learn more about asylum." I have a couple other similar ads where I just change up the text a bit. Using these ads, I get about 120 to 180 new likes on my Facebook page per week.

### *Facebook Live*

Once you have a significant number of followers, start a regular Facebook Live program. Facebook Live videos are real-time video posts where people can post comments, which you will see as they are posted. The live videos you create will appear in your followers' News Feeds, and since Facebook Live is still relatively new, Facebook promotes it by bumping it higher in people's feeds, which means your followers will likely see your video if they are on Facebook while you are doing it.

To create a Facebook Live post, you will need to do it from a device that has a camera and a microphone, such as your phone, tablet, or computer. Write a post to get started, and then press the Live Video button. Once you press that button, you will begin live streaming, so start talking! In my experience, it usually takes about 5 to 10 minutes to really get people watching, so start with a topic. As you are streaming, you will be able to see on the screen how many people are watching, and you will be able to read their comments as they come in.

Doing a Facebook Live post may seem awkward at first, especially if you are not comfortable speaking in public. I pretend I am in an actual consultation and talking to someone face-to-face to help feel more natural. Remember, your viewers are watching you for a reason and are typically very thankful for your help. So don't worry if you get tongue-tied or stumble at first. It will get easier with time.

Here are my top tips for a Facebook Live post:

- Start with a topic, but pause every minute or so to tell people to post their questions.
- Repeat your contact information many times throughout the video.
- Address people by name. For example: "We have a new question. Fred Miller asked . . ."
- At the end of the post, tell your viewers how much you enjoyed answering their questions and that you look forward to doing it again soon. Repeat your contact information and urge them to set up a consultation if they want one-on-one advice.
- Have someone answering your phones during your Facebook Live post and for about an hour afterward.
- Offer a discount on the consultation if someone calls during or within an hour after the Facebook Live post and mentions it.
- Create a weekly program on the same day and at the same time so your followers know when they'll hear from you. Feel free to change the date and time as you figure out the best way to target your followers.

After my first Facebook Live post, I already saw an increase in calls from potential clients. Now it has become a major part of my marketing strategy, and my consultations per week have doubled. Facebook Live is an amazing tool, especially if your target market is active on Facebook. Try it on a weekly basis for at least a month to see what happens with your business.

## Instagram

Instagram is all about images and is a creative way to market your business. Instagram has exploded over the last few years, and now one billion people use it every month. That's a lot of potential business for you and your firm if you can leverage Instagram in the right ways.

When deciding whether to use Instagram, think about your target audience—71 percent of Instagram users are under age 35, and 75 percent of teens use Instagram, so if you have a younger ideal client, this may be a good platform for you.

To use Instagram to really grow your client base, you need to tell a story through photos and videos. You will start by posting a photo, but then you need to create a caption that expands on that story. Think about who your ideal clients are and what they want to hear from you. Then, try and encompass that in your caption, together with the photo.

For example, I recently posted a selfie of myself at the office on a weekend. My caption said, "It's Sunday, but I'm working hard in our Bellevue, WA, office. I love meeting new clients, no matter what day of the week it is! Between appointments, I'm working on a VAWA case for a Latina woman who has suffered serious abuse from her U.S. citizen husband. I feel so fortunate to be able to help her change her life. Hopefully, she will soon get her permanent residence!"

This caption is designed to show my followers the following:

1. I am in my new, Bellevue, Washington, office, open for business.
2. I work with Latinos.
3. I work with victims of abuse.
4. I help people get their permanent residence.
5. I work hard on the weekends.

One simple photo, along with a carefully worded caption, sent the exact message I wanted to get across to my clients.

Something I've noticed when using Instagram is that people tend to respond better to actual photos of me or something work-related, such as a stack of cases, rather than stock photos. This applies even when the stock photo is relevant, such as an American flag on the Fourth of July. People come to Instagram to see real people and real art, not for stock photos and quotes. So if you plan to go big on Instagram, get ready to take some photos and put yourself out there.

Another important element of Instagram is hashtags. Instagram users not only follow other users, but they also follow specific hashtags. By carefully using hashtags, you can end up in the feeds of individuals who have never heard of you before but who may fall squarely into your target market. Before you start posting on Instagram, do a little research. Figure out what hashtags your target client is following that are also relevant in some way to your firm.

## YouTube

YouTube is a great way to promote yourself and your firm, and to help your website rise in the Google rankings.

When you start creating YouTube videos, you do not need the fanciest equipment, especially since you're broke. To be honest, the camera on your cell phone or tablet will do the trick—just make sure you can set it up stably so it doesn't shake while you're filming.

When you're ready to film, find a place with a neutral background. If you have an office space with a blank or simply decorated wall, that will work. Another option is to sit at a desk and film at a wider angle to show more of the office. I filmed most of my first YouTube videos against an off-white wall in my living room, and that worked just fine. Play around with the camera to see what works, and make sure you have plenty of lighting so the video is clear and doesn't have too many shadows.

Before filming, prepare an outline of what you want to say. As with other forms of social media, keep your target client in mind and tailor your video accordingly. Address topics that are of interest to your target client, and keep the video relatively short (preferably less than 10 minutes), so the viewer doesn't get bored.

Tips for filming your videos:

- If possible, when you film, enlist someone to tell you where to stand, how the lighting looks, and so on.
- Let your personality come through in the video—this makes it more interesting to watch.
- Give out your contact information in the video.
- Save time by filming multiple videos in one session.

After you film the video, you should edit it before posting to YouTube. There are a few free editing programs you can use, including Windows Movie Maker, which comes with most computers that have Windows. Another low-cost program is Open Broadcaster Software (OBS). Both of these programs are fairly basic, but at this point you don't need to do anything fancy.

When editing, trim the beginning and end of the video to delete any empty space before and after your content. You also want to enhance the sound, if possible. Depending on the capabilities of the program you use, play around with the brightness and contrast of the video.

Another option is to add text to the video so that viewers can follow along with important points. Add at least your contact information as text in the video so potential clients can easily contact you to set up a consultation.

After your video is edited, upload it to YouTube. If you haven't created a YouTube channel for your firm yet, do it now. When you are logged in to your YouTube channel, press the movie camera button in the upper right corner of the screen, select "Upload," and follow the steps to upload your new video. Create a title and add your contact information in the description.

After you upload your video to YouTube, you will get a link to share the video. Post that link on your other social media platforms and embed it into your website, if possible. If you recorded multiple videos on the same day, post one and save the rest so you can post a new one every month or so. This will make your hard work last longer.

## Tinder—Just Kidding!

Unless you can make it work and still comply with your state bar's ethical rules. Then, by all means, go for it!

## Yelp

I use Yelp all the time. I use it if I'm looking for a new restaurant, a tailor, a hair salon, and so many other things. Why not use Yelp to look for an attorney?

I didn't have a Yelp account for a long time for a couple reasons. First, I was afraid of bad reviews, and second, I didn't think my client base, most of whom do not speak English, would ever use Yelp. But a colleague recently convinced me otherwise, so I just started developing my Yelp account.

To develop my Yelp page, I started directly asking certain clients to write reviews. In my practice, I am using Yelp to target high-literacy immigration clients, such as companies seeking to hire highly skilled immigrants, so those are the types of clients I am asking to write reviews.

In your practice, think about which of your clients, if any, would use Yelp, and ask those clients to start writing reviews. If you don't have any clients yet, that's fine, just get the account set up and start asking clients as they come. If you previously worked for another firm, you could contact past clients there to ask them to write a review. If you did good work on their cases, they will likely be happy to do it.

### CHAPTER CHECKLIST: BRING IN BUSINESS

- ❒ **Establish your target market.** Before you even start trying to get clients, make sure you know exactly who to market to. Be as specific as possible.
- ❒ **Create a networking plan.** Where are you going to network? How often? What do you want to achieve while networking? Answer all of these questions and then get some networking events on your calendar.

- ❒ **Volunteer.** Take on a pro bono case, volunteer at a one-time workshop, or find an organization where you can volunteer regularly. The idea is to get your name out there, help others, and keep your skills sharp.
- ❒ **Use your pen and your word to get noticed.** Find speaking engagements. Write legal articles. Does your practice area or bar have a newsletter you can submit articles to or conferences you can volunteer to speak at? You might need to put the effort in networking and volunteering before these opportunities open up to you, but start looking into your options.
- ❒ **Get on social media.** ASAP. Social media opens a whole world of marketing opportunities. Figure out where your ideal client hangs out on social media, create an account there, and get active.

CHAPTER 5

# Case Management: How to Keep Track of All Your New Cases

**OUTLINE**

**Case-Management Software**
**What to Track**
**Chapter Checklist: Stay Organized**

If you followed the tips and suggestions from previous chapters, you are starting to generate new business for your law firm. You may have also brought clients with you from a prior position at another firm. Either way, as soon as you have your first client, start a system of managing your cases. Whether you have 5 or 500 cases, make sure nothing slips through the cracks, and having a carefully planned system in place from the get-go is the best way to do that.

## CASE-MANAGEMENT SOFTWARE

### Google Drive

Once again, Google proves to be an excellent product for the business owner on a budget. Google Drive is a cloud-based program that allows users to create folders and documents that link to other Google products, such as Gmail, Google Calendar, and Google Contacts.

Although Google Drive is a free product (our favorite!), Google also offers Google Drive for Business, which starts at $6 per month and offers increased security. If you are already paying $6 per month for a Gmail or Google Voice account, this is included. Basically, when you purchase one Google product, you get them all.

Even though it is always tempting to go with the free product, I suggest going with Google Drive for Business to ensure you are complying with the ethical rules related to client confidentiality. That peace of mind is worth the extra $6 per month, even for the broke attorney. Additionally, Google Drive for Business does a great job of linking all your Google products together, which helps streamline the different aspects of your business. You can even add your logo in place of the Google logo on the different products you use through Google business, which creates a more professional look.

### Setting Up Google Drive as a Case Management Program

To get started with Google Drive, create an account. Go to https://gsuite.google.com/products/drive/ and click Get Started. Then, just follow the prompts. If you already have a Google account for your business, simply log in and open Drive.

After you create your account, it's time to get organized. Think about your main organizational needs in your business, and start creating folders based on those needs.

For my law firm, I created the following primary folders:

1. Admin: Used for saving all non-law-related documents, such as accounting, business licenses, and so on
2. Case Admin: Used for saving all law-related documents that don't pertain to a specific case, such as templates and samples, general topical research, and new case law
3. Marketing: Used for all marketing-related documentation, including written work, outlines for speaking engagements, YouTube videos, and so on
4. Cases: Used for all cases, past, present, and potential

Again, these are all *primary* folders. Within each of these folders, I got even more specific with subfolders. For example, in the Cases folder, I included subfolders titled, "Potential Cases," "Current Cases," and "Closed Cases." And within those subfolders, I created additional folders for each case.

The folders I created for my law firm are only an example of what you can do for your business in Google Drive. The most important thing is to create a system that works for you and stick to it.

## MyCase

Once you start making more money and your client base has grown, you might be ready to graduate to a software specifically designed for case management. Although I started out with Google Drive and really liked it, I started using MyCase when I switched from flat-fee billing to hourly billing about a year and a half into my practice. If I hadn't switched to hourly billing, I would probably still use Google Drive, but now that I've made the switch, I'm happy I did.

MyCase is fairly inexpensive case management software that keeps all the different aspects of each case in one spot. Once you create a case file for a particular case, MyCase will create multiple helpful tabs for that case, including Calendar, Documents, Tasks, Notes, and Messages. MyCase also allows you to create invoices, it has a timer to track the time you spend working on each case (you should do this even if you don't practice hourly billing), and it allows you to link to your email.

Another huge benefit of MyCase is that you can grant your clients access to their files. You still have control over what documents they see, but giving clients access allows them a secure portal to upload new documentation and ask you case-sensitive questions.

MyCase also has great customer service. They typically respond to questions within 24 hours—often sooner—and they always follow up to ensure any fixes are working properly. Additionally, they provide many different training videos to help new users familiarize themselves with the software.

MyCase offers an excellent product at a reasonable price. Again, I suggest starting with Google Drive for free and waiting until you absolutely need (and can afford) a more advanced case management software before switching to MyCase. When you decide to do so, start with a 30-day trial by going to www.mycase.com/free-trial to make sure you like it.

# WHAT TO TRACK

Aside from monitoring your cases, there are many other things you should track in your law firm to ensure you stay on top of things, continue to grow, and make more money. The more you know about your business, the more money you will ultimately bring in.

## Case Fees and Payments

There are many successful attorneys who make a lot less money than they could, even though they have a lot of cases. This isn't because they charge less or differently; it's because they don't track their clients' payments and regularly follow up when a client is behind on paying their bill. A close friend of mine had this problem in her practice, and as soon as she began tracking client payments and following up on late payments, her revenue more than doubled. So if you're going to carefully track one thing in your business, it should be the payment of your legal fees.

If you just opened your practice and are using Google Drive to manage your cases, the easiest way to track payments is in Excel or with Google Sheets. On the document, list the client's name, fee structure, total amount owed, total amount paid, amount of next payment, and due date of next payment. Make the payment due date the same for each client, perhaps the 30th of the month, to make it easier for you to track.

Check out the sample spreadsheet here, and find a full template in Appendix C:

**FEE TRACKING SPREADSHEET**

| Client Name | Fee Structure | Total Fee | Total Paid | Next Payment Amount | Next Payment Due |
|---|---|---|---|---|---|
| John Doe | Flat | $10,000 | $4,000 | $500 | 7/31/20 |
| Suzie Cue | Hourly | N/A | $2,500 | $632 (invoiced) | 7/31/20 |
| | | | | | |
| | | | | | |
| | | | | | |
| | | | | | |
| | | | | | |
| | | | | | |

Update your spreadsheet whenever a new client retains you, you send out an invoice, or a client makes a payment. Every month, go through your spreadsheet to see who is overdue on their bill. Even though this part is difficult for many attorneys, you then need to call all clients who are overdue to remind them to pay. You will be surprised how many actually pay and what a difference this makes on your bottom line.

## Referral Sources

Tracking referral sources is the best way to determine where you generate the most business, and then focus your efforts. When I first started my practice, I volunteered at multiple nonprofits, I actively participated in multiple networking groups, I took pro bono cases, I created YouTube videos, and I was active on social media. As my caseload grew, I no longer had time for so many activities, and I had to decide what to cut. Because I carefully track the source of all new clients, I was able to look back and determine which activities generate the most business for my law firm and eliminate those that don't.

Just like tracking your payments, you can track your referrals using Excel or Google Sheets. However, with this one, you can get really fancy with it, making tallies auto-populate, creating color-coded graphs, and so on. "But, Lauren," you may be saying to yourself, "not all of us are Excel geniuses like you clearly are." Wrong! I am not an Excel genius, my husband is, and I milk his skills for all they're worth (*#marriage*). Fortunately for you, I'm including this awesome spreadsheet in Appendix D, as well as making it available for download at https://ambar.org/startalawfirm.

In the meantime, look at this sample. The referral sources will change for your own firm, but this is a great way to track your referrals and focus your marketing efforts in the areas that bring the most returns.

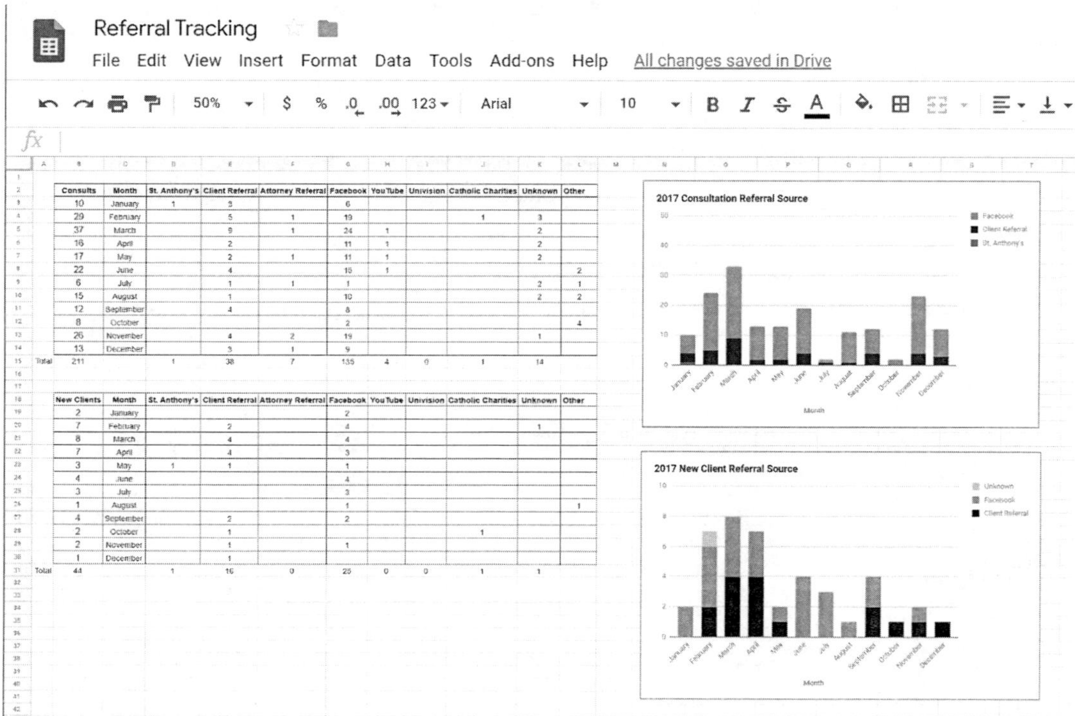


| Consults | Month | St. Anthony's | Client Referral | Attorney Referral | Facebook | YouTube | Univision | Catholic Charities | Unknown | Other |
|---|---|---|---|---|---|---|---|---|---|---|
| 10 | January | 1 | 3 | | 6 | | | | | |
| 29 | February | | 5 | 1 | 19 | | | 1 | 3 | |
| 37 | March | | 9 | 1 | 24 | 1 | | | 2 | |
| 16 | April | | 2 | | 11 | 1 | | | 2 | |
| 17 | May | | 2 | 1 | 11 | 1 | | | 2 | |
| 22 | June | | 4 | | 15 | 1 | | | | 2 |
| 6 | July | | 1 | 1 | 1 | | | | 2 | 1 |
| 15 | August | | 1 | | 10 | | | | 2 | 2 |
| 12 | September | | 4 | | 8 | | | | | |
| 8 | October | | | | 2 | | | | | 4 |
| 26 | November | | 4 | 2 | 19 | | | | 1 | |
| 13 | December | | 3 | 1 | 9 | | | | | |
| Total 211 | | 1 | 38 | 7 | 135 | 4 | 0 | 1 | 14 | |

| New Clients | Month | St. Anthony's | Client Referral | Attorney Referral | Facebook | YouTube | Univision | Catholic Charities | Unknown | Other |
|---|---|---|---|---|---|---|---|---|---|---|
| 2 | January | | | | 2 | | | | | |
| 7 | February | | 2 | | 4 | | | | 1 | |
| 8 | March | | 4 | | 4 | | | | | |
| 7 | April | | 4 | | 3 | | | | | |
| 3 | May | 1 | 1 | | 1 | | | | | |
| 4 | June | | | | 4 | | | | | |
| 3 | July | | | | 3 | | | | | |
| 1 | August | | | | 1 | | | | | 1 |
| 4 | September | | 2 | | 2 | | | | | |
| 2 | October | | 1 | | | | | 1 | | |
| 2 | November | | 1 | | 1 | | | | | |
| 1 | December | | 1 | | | | | | | |
| Total 44 | | 1 | 16 | 0 | 25 | 0 | 0 | 1 | 1 | |

## Types of Cases

If you work in more than one practice area or subarea, you should track the type of cases you have in your practice. This will help you learn what type of case generates the most business for you and will allow you to focus your efforts when marketing. This is also important information as you look for speaking engagements and writing opportunities, because you will be able to give specific data to back up your purported experience.

For example, even though I exclusively practice immigration law, one area I tend to focus on is defensive asylum cases. Therefore, I focus much of my Facebook marketing on asylum applications. In my Facebook Live posts, I almost always spend some time talking about asylum, and when I go to conferences and take continuing legal education classes, I try to learn as much as possible about asylum. Narrowing my focus this way has allowed me to grow my practice and bring in business I otherwise would not have pursued if I were unaware of the practice-area statistics in my firm.

## Time Spent on Tasks

Everyone HATES tracking their time. It can be stressful. However, for your business, eschew all your previous feelings about tracking your time, and think of it as a way to focus and grow your business. Now, you are not tracking your time to meet a billable hour requirement, but to see where you spend most of your time and find ways to reduce wasted time to become more efficient. The ultimate goal is to work less.

If you are using Google Drive or a similar program for case management, you can track your time in a spreadsheet. Create columns labeled "Date," "Case," "Task," and "Time." In the case column, put "Admin" or "Marketing" when the task is not related to a case, but try to be consistent. Look at the following example, and also check out the template at Appendix E. You can also download a fill-in-the-blank version at https://ambar.org/startalawfirm.

This spreadsheet should be the first document you open when you begin each workday. Track everything you do for your business from this point forward.

| Codes for Services | | Client Number | Client/Case | Date | Services Performed | Time |
|---|---|---|---|---|---|---|
| 9999 | Admin | | | | | |
| 9998 | Marketing | | | | | |
| 9997 | Networking | | | | | |
| 9996 | Volunteer | | | | | |
| 0 | Potential Client | | | | | |
| 9999 | Admin | | | | | |
| 9998 | Marketing | | | | | |
| 9997 | Networking | | | | | |
| 9996 | Volunteer | | | | | |
| 0 | Potential Client | | | | | |

When tracking your time, enter information into your spreadsheet as soon as you finish a task. If you wait until the end of the day, you might forget a task or two. The most common way to break down time is into increments of 1⁄10 of an hour, or by every six minutes. If you purchased a case management program that has a time-tracking function, there's no need to create your own spreadsheet. Just use the tracker that came with the program.

As your firm gets going, analyze the data from your time tracking on a monthly basis. Figure out how much time you're spending on certain tasks or case types. Are there areas where you should be more efficient? Do you need to raise your fees for certain types of cases? Would it be more cost-effective to hire someone to help with certain tasks? Use this timesheet as a tool to streamline your business.

## Deadlines

One of the most important things when working on cases is complying with deadlines. Miss a deadline, and you could end all options for relief for your client. Miss enough deadlines and screw up enough cases, and you could get disbarred. Deadlines are no joke, and you must have a system in place for tracking them.

The simplest way to track deadlines is by using a calendar. If you opted for a case management program, the calendar will come with it. And if you decided to use something free, like Google, you will also have a calendar. From now on, it is imperative that you use this calendar. Sync it to your phone. Set up a reminder. Open it as soon as you start your computer each day.

To avoid missing deadlines, create a system that works well for your firm and ensures nothing gets missed and everything gets added to the calendar. If you are struggling to create your own system, here is a simple one for you:

1. The moment you learn of a filing deadline, a hearing date, a client meeting, and so on, add it to the calendar.
2. If you are waiting to receive notice of a deadline, set yourself a task to follow up each week to ensure the notice does not get lost, causing you to inadvertently miss a deadline.
3. Set reminders on the calendar. For anything that requires prepwork, such as a filing deadline, set reminders two weeks before the deadline, one week before the deadline, two days before the deadline, and the day of the deadline. For things that don't require much prep, set a reminder for one day before the deadline.
4. At the beginning of each day, review your calendar for the next two weeks, just to ensure nothing slips through the cracks.

Follow this simple system religiously, and you will not miss any deadlines. If you have staff, require your staff to do the same. You should maintain a no-missed-deadlines policy in your office.

## CHAPTER CHECKLIST: STAY ORGANIZED

- ❒ **Select a software.** Determine whether to invest in a case management program (which can be a bit pricey when you're broke) or use a free option like Google Drive. Create an account in whichever you select.
- ❒ **Create a spreadsheet to track your cases.** This spreadsheet allows you to quickly see an overview of all the cases you are handling.
- ❒ **Create a spreadsheet to track case fees and payments.** This is super important to help you stay organized and ensure you get paid for your work. It also allows you to keep clear records in case someone files a bar complaint against you. Use this spreadsheet diligently.
- ❒ **Create a spreadsheet to track your referrals.** This is key as you start building your client base. After a few months or a year of tracking, you will have a clear picture of where to focus your marketing efforts.
- ❒ **Create a spreadsheet to track your time.** You can do this quickly in Excel or Google Sheets. Or, if you invested in a case management program, set up the time-tracking feature.
- ❒ **Create an organizational system.** Set up folders. Create a consistent way to label things, and write it down.
- ❒ **Go digital.** Get an efficient scanner if your virtual office service doesn't provide one. Make sure you have a strong digital system for organizing everything (see previous task). Add a clause to your retainer agreement that says you will keep digital files only.

CHAPTER **6**

# Getting Paid

**OUTLINE**



Your firm is running efficiently, you have new clients coming in, and you're working hard on their cases. But none of this matters if you aren't getting paid. In this section, we'll talk about the different types of fee arrangements and how to ensure your clients actually pay you.

## TYPES OF FEE ARRANGEMENTS

There are a few different fee structures that attorneys typically use when setting up agreements with their clients. The most common are flat fees, hourly fees, and contingent fees. When deciding on your preferred fee structure, check the ethical rules in your state to ensure you are complying with any restrictions on fee agreements, as some practice areas are restricted from certain types of fee structures. Also, keep in mind the type of cases you handle and your client base, and really think about the structure that will best work with your practice.

### Flat Fee

A flat fee is when the attorney charges a specific, total fee for work done on the case. Flat fees are typically used for straightforward cases in which the attorney can reasonably estimate the amount of time he or she will spend on the matter.

## What Are the Benefits of Flat Fees?

Simplicity. Because flat fees are set, they require less management than other types of fee structures, which means you don't need to track your time on the case. For attorneys who hate tracking time, this is a huge benefit.

Clients also like flat fees, because they know, from the beginning, how much they are going to pay the attorney. This usually prevents disagreements over fees and allows both the attorney and the client to plan ahead financially.

## What Are the Difficulties of Flat Fees?

Although flat fees are simple, the attorney may not always get fully compensated for the work they perform on the case. Although a case may seem simple on the surface, complications can arise, resulting in more work for the attorney. And unless the retainer agreement between the attorney and the client is carefully written to account for such surprises, the attorney may be on the hook for additional work.

Even though flat fees are simpler than hourly fees, the attorney may not always be allowed to put the fee directly into their operating account upon receipt. The ethical rules of many states require an attorney to leave fees in trust until they have reached certain milestones in the case. However, read the rules of your state carefully, as you may be able to draft language in your retainer agreement that allows you to put funds directly into your operating account upon receipt. This is one area where flat fees aren't always as straightforward as they seem.

## Tips for Using a Flat-Fee Payment System

I used flat fees for the first year and a half of my practice, then switched to hourly, and then ultimately switched back to flat fees. Here are some tips to make flat fees work for you:

- Carefully draft your retainer agreement. Include language to protect you in case you must do additional, unexpected work on the case.
- Require clients to make a deposit before starting the case. Even if you set up a payment plan, this shows they are invested.
- If you allow your clients to have a payment plan, rather than paying everything up front, set the same due date for all of your clients. This makes financial tracking easier.
- Unless your client has paid the full fee amount up front, send regular invoices.
- Track your hours to determine a reasonable fee for each case type, based on the amount of work you typically do. Even if that's a high fee, charge it!

Flat fees are a great option if you're unsure about trust accounting and want to start off with something a little simpler or if your practice consists of straightforward, predictable cases. They are also a good option if your clients are individuals, not businesses, who may have a harder time wrapping their minds around other fee structures.

## Hourly Fees

Under an hourly fee structure, the attorney will charge the client for each hour (or portion of an hour) that they work on the case. For example, if the attorney's fee is $100 per hour and they work five hours, the fee will be $500. Some lawyers charge different fees for different types of work (legal research versus a court appearance). In addition, lawyers working in large firms typically have different fee scales with more senior members charging higher fees than young associates or paralegals.

### *What Are the Benefits of Hourly Fees?*

The main benefit of charging an hourly fee is that you get paid for the work you do, which is fair to you and the client. If a case moves along quickly and the client is efficient in getting documents to you, you will do less work and the client will pay less money. It's a win-win. And if a case drags out for years or the client refuses to cooperate, you will be compensated for the extra time you put into the case.

Additionally, charging on an hourly basis makes your revenue more consistent and predictable. For example, if you charge $250 per hour and your legal assistant charges $150 per hour, and you each work 20 billable hours per week, you know that you will earn $8,000 per week. This knowledge makes it much easier to prepare for expenses and regulate the flow of work.

### *What Are the Difficulties of Hourly Fees?*

The most difficult thing for many attorneys to do is track their hours. Once you switch to hourly billing, you will need to track every minute you and your staff work on a case. You will also need to review your and your staff's time entries to decide what work should be billed and what work shouldn't. For example, I typically don't bill for opening and setting up the initial case file, and I do not bill for work done as a result of a mistake by me or my staff.

Additionally, it can be difficult to manage client expectations. Since you aren't quoting a set fee, like you would with a flat-fee system, the client does not know how much he or she will ultimately pay for your services. This can get tricky if you end up billing more than the client anticipated, and you will need to back up the bill with a detailed outline of the tasks you performed on the case.

### *Setting Up Fee Payments Under an Hourly Fee Structure*

There are a few different ways to set up fee payments for clients. Some attorneys require a large retainer up front, work off that retainer, and then require another large retainer after the funds fall below a certain amount. In this scenario, the attorney repeats the process of requesting large retainers until the case is complete.

Other attorneys require a retainer up front and then have their clients make monthly payments based on an estimated fee amount. In this scenario, the attorney does not request more than the agreed-upon monthly payment, even if more work was completed than necessary to cover the funds.

Some attorneys do not require an up-front payment at all, but simply bill the client monthly or bimonthly for the work that was done. This seems to work well for high-income clients, but it is more difficult for low-income clients, who often end up not paying.

One method is to require a large retainer up front plus indefinite monthly payments. You can give your clients an estimate, but they are still responsible for making the monthly payment into trust for the duration of the case or until the total balance is paid off, whichever is longer. This method makes it easy for the client to budget for their monthly payment.

The issue I ultimately had with hourly fees was that clients really couldn't wrap their mind around how it worked and would get frustrated that they had to keep paying and paying, without a definite end date. This resulted in a lot of time wasted in meetings in which we just discussed billing.

### *Tips for Using an Hourly Fee System*

I learned a lot in the time I spent billing hourly. I made mistakes and improvements, and I now have some good tips for making hourly billing as easy as possible:

- Have a good retainer agreement that outlines the fee structure.
- Get a case management program to track your time. MyCase is great.
- Require clients to make a deposit before starting the case. This way, you will have funds to draw from as you begin work.
- Explain to clients how trust accounting works. Be very clear and give an estimate that is higher than what you think it will actually be.
- Tell clients that if there is money left over in their account at the end of the case, you will return it to them. They love that.
- Send clients a monthly invoice that includes all your time entries so they can see where their money is going.
- As you are working, try to pace yourself so there is always some money left in the client's trust account. This isn't always possible, but it's a good goal.

Although I have switched back to flat fees, I learned a lot from hourly billing. Most importantly, I learned how much my typical cases actually cost, based on the hours I invest in them. This allowed me to switch back to flat fees and charge a much more accurate fee.

If you are on the fence about whether to do hourly billing, just try it. If anything, you will gain valuable insights in the process.

## Contingency Fees

I have never dealt with contingency fees myself, so I reached out to an amazing employment law attorney, Jacob M. Small of J. Madison PLC, to give me all the details. Before starting J. Madison PLC, Jacob worked at the White House, where he was a member of the vice president's legal team. He worked to help the president and vice president identify and address some of the nation's most important legal issues, including those affecting minorities and women in the workplace. Jacob also worked for the Department of Justice and the Commonwealth's attorney in Loudoun County, Virginia, where he prosecuted criminal cases.

Jacob knows his stuff, and here's what he has to say about contingency fees.[1]

With a contingent fee representation agreement, you perform legal services for your client in exchange for a percentage of an anticipated recovery while forgoing an hourly or flat fee. A contingency fee model may be appropriate for the plaintiff's lawyer serving a population that is likely to possess valuable claims but no or limited ability to pay fees. Attorneys who engage in contingency representation accept the risk of receiving no fees when their clients' claims are defeated. But they also see the potential for large fees when their efforts are successful.

### What Are the Benefits of Contingency Fees?

There are two primary benefits of the contingency model. First, contingency fees allow you to offer important legal services to populations who might otherwise have no access to representation. In this way, the contingency fee helps increase access to justice for less-affluent communities.

Second, with contingency fees, you may earn more than you might with an hourly or flat fee, in exchange for accepting risk. If you are representing clients in litigation with valuable claims, then you might start to see the contingency model as more attractive than an hourly or flat fee model, because of the potential upside.

### What Are the Difficulties of Contingency Fees?

The risks inherent to the lawyer who offers contingency representation cannot not be overstated. When you agree to prosecute clients' claims in exchange for a speculative future fee, you are placing a bet. Undoubtedly, some or many of those bets will fail, especially early in your career. Before deciding to represent clients pursuant to a contingency fee agreement, you should be prepared for the financial and emotional consequences of writing off hundreds of thousands of dollars' worth of work should your efforts fail. No one is successful all the time, and you must appreciate that a contingency practice is about building and nurturing a portfolio of cases, some of which will fail to deliver a return on your investment.

### Costs in a Contingency Fee Practice

If you are building a contingency fee–based practice, consider how you will approach paying litigation costs. The first place to start when considering costs is

[1] The author is grateful to Jacob M. Small for contributing his discussion of contingency fees to this book.

your state's conflict of interest rules regarding financial assistance to clients. ABA Model Rule 1.8(e) and subparts provides as follows:

> (e) A lawyer shall not provide financial assistance to a client in connection with pending or contemplated litigation, except that:
>
> (1) a lawyer may advance court costs and expenses of litigation, the repayment of which may be contingent on the outcome of the matter; and
>
> (2) a lawyer representing an indigent client may pay court costs and expenses of litigation on behalf of the client.

If your state follows this basic structure, then take note: you may not pay your clients' costs for them, even if you are representing them on a contingency fee basis. You may, however, advance those costs, and you will likely find good enough reason to do so in some cases. For the plaintiff's lawyer, litigation is an attempt to liquidate a speculative investment through the investment of time and money. You will not be able to liquidate all your clients' claims without hiring court reporters to take depositions and generate transcripts, expert witnesses for reports and testimony, or various consultants to assist you along the way. These professionals require payment up front, and you should carefully consider whether you will advance these costs to your client.

When you get involved with a case, you won't know enough about its strengths and weaknesses to know whether it makes business sense to advance any costs. You'll likely face the same dilemma at the outset of representation. For this reason, your agreement with your client should make clear that the client bears full responsibility for paying all costs (as the ethics rules require) but that you reserve the right, in appropriate cases, to advance to your client some or all costs with their consent. You need the ability to support a good case that needs reasonable investment, but you also need the ability to decline to invest your finances when the investment appears poor or when you cannot afford to do so. After setting up your agreement in this way, be realistic when considering whether a specific investment is appropriate. And beware of the sunk cost fallacy: do not throw good money after bad!

## *Developing a Contingent-Fee Structure*

As you put together your contingent fee model, consider the various stages in the life cycle of your clients' cases. A case might settle during your initial investigation. It could also settle after an initial investigation, but before the parties have expended much time, money, or effort in litigation. On the other hand, some cases will require hundreds of hours of work and will only be resolved by a judge or jury's verdict after summary judgment. And other cases will need to survive various appeals before a fee is paid. You will likely find it appropriate to structure your contingency fee agreements with the case life cycle in mind. Draft an agreement that provides you with two important rights: the right to walk away and the right to require an increased fee. Let's discuss each of these rights in turn.

First, you need the ability to end your representation in cases that appear weaker today than they did when you offered representation. You can always withdraw when doing so is appropriate under the ethics rules, but it may make more sense to limit the services offered to discrete stages in a case's life cycle.

In my practice, I use different agreements for different stages of my clients' cases: (1) initial investigation and negotiation, (2) litigation before a government agency, (3) litigation before a court, and (4) litigation of an appeal. When I complete my initial investigation, I determine if there's a good faith basis for asserting a claim. If so, I attempt to negotiate my clients' claims to resolution, but I am not yet obligated to initiate or prosecute litigation. If those negotiations fail, I have performed all services promised to the client, and I can walk away from the case if necessary. But if the case still appears viable, I can offer my client a new agreement for the next stage in the case's life cycle.

Second, you need the ability to increase your fee as the complexity, commitment, and investment in your cases increases. Build a fee structure that pays you an initial percentage for cases settled with minimal work and increased fees for cases that take more time and investment. I accomplish this in my practice by charging one fee for an investigation and negotiation and a higher fee for litigation. Because the first agreement my client signs does not obligate me to conduct litigation, only the lower fee applies to that agreement. Nevertheless, that initial agreement lays out my fee structure, so that clients are adequately informed at the beginning of the representation. You may also find it appropriate to increase fees if you make a financial investment or if you must prepare for or conduct a trial.

### *Tips for Using a Contingency Fee System*

Here are some useful tips to consider as you put together your contingency fee–based practice:

- Get paid. Structure your agreement with your client and your client's agreement with a settling defendant so that your fees are paid directly to you, on the client's behalf. You don't want to chase contingency fees that your client has already spent.
- Protect your investment. If your state allows you to assert an attorneys' lien in the event you are dismissed, include the client's consent to your assertion of such a lien in your fee agreement. Hopefully you won't need to assert one, but don't let there be doubt about whether you can.
- Avoid unpaid follow-up work. Consider inserting into your agreements an hourly or flat fee for nonessential work that your client wants you to perform after the case is resolved. For example, you will likely get calls or emails from clients whose cases settled months or years ago, seeking advice about tax

payments, documents, or other miscellaneous matters. Your life will be much easier if everyone knows in advance that your responses to these inquiries will be paid at a specific rate.

- Screen your cases. The best way to ensure that you don't lose money on contingency work is to avoid getting involved in bad cases. Learning to identify good cases takes time, but when in doubt, trust your gut. Normally, if you see a red flag, don't ignore it.
- Don't bite off more than you can chew. The new plaintiff's attorney should be wary of getting in over his or her head. Just like a criminal lawyer's first case should probably not be a capital murder case, your first years in practice as a plaintiff's lawyer should be focused on cases of an appropriate size and complexity. By recognizing the limits of your experience, you can begin building a profitable portfolio of cases appropriate to your skills. As time passes and you gain experience, push yourself by seeking out more complex, and potentially more lucrative, opportunities.
- Push your cases. With a contingency fee–based practice, you can be your own worst enemy. You need to find good cases and push them hard to resolution. If you fail to do this, you won't be in practice for very long. But if you can find good cases and work them, you'll be rewarded with a satisfying career and a handsome return on your investment.

## INVOICES

An attorney I know was signing multiple new cases each week, doing excellent work for her clients, and becoming very well known in the community. Despite all this, she wasn't making much of a profit in her law firm. She had been neglecting the accounting side of her business, and one day she decided to buckle down and send an invoice to all clients who owed money on their case. Within two weeks, her clients had paid her close to $20,000, just in late payments. After this, she swore she would never neglect to send out invoices again.

As attorneys, we often get wrapped up in the legal work and assume our clients will make their payments as scheduled. WRONG! Without an invoice nagging at them, clients often forget (sometimes willfully) to pay their bill. By setting up a system for sending and following up on invoices, you will ensure that your clients make their payments on time and in full.

### Wave Accounting

There are a few different programs you can use to prepare invoices, but Wave (www.waveapps.com) is great and it's free! You can use it for all your accounting and invoicing needs. It is straightforward, easy to use, and has a pretty good forum for finding answers if you get stuck on something.

Wave Invoices allow you to create template invoices that you can alter slightly for each new client. On the template, you can add your logo, any standard language or disclaimers, and even template fees. Additionally, you can set up recurring invoices for any client who is on a payment plan. You can set Wave to automatically email the recurring invoices to your client on a preselected day of the month, week, or year. This makes it incredibly easy for you to focus on other aspects of your firm, knowing that your invoice will automatically go out.

Once a client makes a payment, add the payment to the invoice, and the payment will automatically be reflected in your transactions on Wave, if you also use Wave for your business accounting. Using Wave for invoicing has been great for my business, and I highly recommend the service.

### Paid Alternatives

There are also many paid invoicing options, some of which may be included with other subscriptions you use. For example, MyCase includes invoicing options. Once I switched to MyCase for my business, I ended up switching my invoicing over to MyCase as well, just to streamline things more. Although I loved Wave, invoicing with MyCase is extremely simple, and I would recommend it to anyone considering a paid case management program.

QuickBooks, a very common accounting program, also comes with an invoicing option. If and when you hire a bookkeeper to handle your books, he or she will likely want to you switch to QuickBooks, since that's the most common program for bookkeeping. At that time, you can start invoicing through QuickBooks, but for now, save your money.

Don't waste your money on a program specifically designed for creating invoices. There are many other programs that implement invoicing along with their primary service. However, if you are considering paying for another service, such as case management software or accounting software, make sure it comes with the added benefit of invoices.

## FOLLOW UP, FOLLOW UP, FOLLOW UP!

Prepared the invoice? Check! Sent it to your client? Check! Received payment? *Crickets chirping*. Although many clients automatically make their payment when you send out the invoice, you will still have some bad or forgetful seeds who won't. That's when you need to follow up.

I get it, following up can be awkward. Until you reach a point in your practice where you can hire an assistant, you're stuck with the task. Here are a few simple tips for making follow-up easier:

- Start with an email. Emails are easier than phone calls, and you can prepare a friendly but firm template email to use with all your clients.
- If the email doesn't work, call your client. Prepare a brief script in advance so you know what you want to say.

- During the call, ask your client when you can expect payment. Be prepared to negotiate a little if the client suggests a date too far in the future.
- Be prepared to explain the different payment options you accept.
- Use an understanding tone, but be firm.
- Set up automatic credit card payments so this doesn't happen again.

To be honest, most of my clients make their payments shortly after that follow-up phone call. Usually they are embarrassed they missed their payment and want to get back on my good side right away. Hopefully you have that type of client, but if not continue following up until the client pays.

If the client refuses to pay, consider withdrawing from the case. Read your ethical rules and follow them carefully on this point. But there's no reason to work for free or allow clients to take advantage of you.

## CREDIT CARDS AND PAYMENT PLANS

Do you hate following up? Another great way to ensure your clients are paying you on time is to set up a regular credit card payments.

I talked about credit card processing companies earlier in the book, and if you haven't set one up yet, do it now. You will make so much more money if you accept credit cards. Recently, we set a new policy in our firm that anyone who wants to pay their bill with a payment plan *must* set up automatic credit card payments. So far, it's been great! The clients are willing to do it because they want a payment plan, and it saves us a ton of time following up. Win, win!

Your primary goal as a business owner is to make money. I know that may sound harsh, especially to those with a passion for humanitarian cases, but you must continually remind yourself that you cannot help your clients unless you take care of yourself first.

### CHAPTER CHECKLIST: MAKE IT RAIN

- ❒ **Determine the fee structure(s) you will use.** Look closely at the types of cases you will handle *and* the types of clients you will work with to determine the fee structure that will serve you best.
- ❒ **Create an account with an accounting program.** Use free software, such as Wave, or another program of your choosing.
- ❒ **Create template invoices.** Your accounting software should provide this, but you will want to tailor the standard language, logo, and other details about your firm.
- ❒ **Set up credit card payments.** Select a service that works well for you and your firm, and set it up. Compare rates and what the service offers.
- ❒ **Follow up.** You will not get paid if you do not send invoices and follow up on late payments. You're broke. You can't afford not to get paid.

CHAPTER 7

# Work Smarter, Not Harder

**OUTLINE**



A lot of attorneys decide to start their own law firm because they're tired of the grind of "big law." Working 10- to 12-hour days gets old really fast and can suck the excitement out of practicing law. As you start your own practice, you may need to put in a lot of work up front to get everything established. However, your ultimate goal should be to make more money while working fewer hours.

In order to work fewer hours while still making bank, you need to start building habits that will allow you to become hyper-organized and hyper-efficient. The idea is to create systems and processes that allow you to do double the work in half the time. That sounds insane, but it is completely doable. This section takes you through tons of efficiency habits that you can implement right now to start creating tons of free time for yourself, while still killing it in your business.

## CREATING YOUR IDEAL WORKWEEK

Before we even dig into all the efficiency habits you are going to implement, start by creating a vision for your ideal workweek. First, just dream. Go somewhere quiet, with no distractions. Close your eyes, and imagine a perfect day. Dream big. You can go anywhere with anyone and do anything. Think about the things you want to do with your free time, and act as if you didn't have to work at all. Write down what you envisioned for your perfect day on the following lines.

Your perfect day:

_________________________________________________________________________________________

_________________________________________________________________________________________

_________________________________________________________________________________________

________________________________________________________________________________________.

Use this vision to shape your reality. Since this book is about starting a law firm, I know you aren't going to stop working completely, but we can use what you visualized to figure out how you can achieve your perfect life with work still in the picture.

Break down your perfect day into specific, real-life elements. For example, did you dream of sleeping in and then wandering down to the beach where you relaxed all day with your significant other, sipping on fruity drinks and reading young adult fiction novels? Or maybe you envisioned getting up early to go for a run, preparing yourself a healthy meal, then taking time to make yourself look amazing before going shopping (at the nice mall, not the sketchy one across town), then meeting up with friends for drinks at a nice bar, and ending the day with a fancy dinner. No matter what you envisioned for your perfect day, you can take elements from that vision that you can incorporate into your real life.

To illustrate this, let's look at the previous examples. For the person relaxing on the beach, some requirements for an ideal life might include sleeping in, having quiet time to relax and read a book, traveling to beach locations, and spending quality time with his or her significant other. For the person who started the day with a run, some daily elements might include taking time in the morning to exercise and eat a good meal, having plenty of time to get ready before going to work, having time and money to shop, checking out nice restaurants, and spending time out with friends.

Thinking back to your vision, what is important to you? Do you want to go out with friends more often? Do you want to spend more time with your family? Do you want to take every Friday off so you can travel, run errands, or just sleep in? Do you want to take a month off every year to travel? Do you want to start work at noon so you can do your own thing in the morning? Think about all the amazing things you want to do outside of work, and list some of them here:

1. _____________________________________________________________________________
2. _____________________________________________________________________________
3. _____________________________________________________________________________
4. _____________________________________________________________________________
5. _____________________________________________________________________________

Add more items to the list if five just isn't enough.

Okay, now that you have a few things you want to do outside of work, it's time to make your firm work around your life, not the other way around. A weekly planner is provided after this section. Fill it in hour by hour, but start with the "life" things first. Leave work last. Remember, you are going to plan your work schedule around your life to make sure you get to enjoy your time in and out of your firm.

As you're doing this, avoid sticking to the traditional nine-to-five mind-set. That is not required now that you have your own firm. Even if your clients think you are working from 9 to 5, you don't have to actually be at the office, working on casework during those hours. While doing this exercise, think outside the box and try your hardest to let go of all the traditional notions of what working in a law firm is like.

In the schedule are samples from a few days of my typical week. Then you will see a blank schedule that you can fill in with your own details. Currently, I work Mondays, Tuesdays, Thursdays, Fridays, and Saturdays. I go into the office on Saturdays because that works really well for my clients and it generates a lot of revenue for my firm, but I take off Wednesdays to focus on myself and do all the non-work things I want to do. During the week, I work shorter, but very efficient days so I don't get burned out and have plenty of time for exercise, relaxation, and personal tasks. I work 20 to 30 hours each week and my firm is thriving—I get lots of business, my clients are happy, my staff enjoys a good work-life balance, and I make a lot of money. So trust me, you can definitely make your firm work around your life.

## SAMPLE SCHEDULE—MONDAY

| | |
|---|---|
| 5:00 a.m. | Wake up, make tea, do yoga. |
| 6:00 a.m. | Me time: read, work on non-firm projects, peruse social media, accomplish random tasks. |
| 7:00 a.m. | The kid wakes up, and morning routine: diaper, clothes, walk dogs while husband gets ready for work. |
| 8:00 a.m. | Send kid and husband off. Shower and get dressed. |
| 9:00 a.m. | Work from home—firm admin tasks. |
| 10:00 a.m. | Work from home—firm admin tasks. |
| 11:00 a.m. | Work from home—firm admin tasks. |
| 12:00 p.m. | Have lunch and check email and staff messages. |

*(continued)*

## SAMPLE SCHEDULE—MONDAY *(continued)*

| | |
|---|---|
| 1:00 p.m. | Work from home—firm admin tasks. |
| 2:00 p.m. | Do any personal computer tasks (travel planning, financial stuff, etc.) or run errands. |
| 3:00 p.m. | Do any personal computer tasks (travel planning, financial stuff, etc.) or run errands. |
| 4:00 p.m. | Check email, then pick up kid from day care. |
| 5:00 p.m. | Walk the dogs with the kid. |
| 6:00 p.m. | Go to the playground with the kid. |
| 7:00 p.m. | Dinner. |
| 8:00 p.m. | Kid in bed. Watch TV with husband. |
| 9:00 p.m. | Get ready for bed and read. |
| 10:00 p.m. | Lights out. |
| 11:00 p.m. | Sleep. |
| 12:00 a.m. | Sleep. |

## SAMPLE SCHEDULE—TUESDAY

| | |
|---|---|
| 5:00 a.m. | Wake up, make tea, do yoga. |
| 6:00 a.m. | Me time: read, work on non-firm projects, peruse social media, accomplish random tasks. |
| 7:00 a.m. | The kid wakes up, and morning routine: diaper, clothes, walk dogs while husband gets ready for work. |
| 8:00 a.m. | Send kid and husband off. Shower and get dressed. |
| 9:00 a.m. | Work from home—review staff work. |
| 10:00 a.m. | Work from home—review staff work. |
| 11:00 a.m. | Work from home—legal writing. |

## SAMPLE SCHEDULE—TUESDAY *(continued)*

| | |
|---|---|
| 12:00 p.m. | Lunch and check email and staff messages. |
| 1:00 p.m. | Work from home—legal writing. |
| 2:00 p.m. | Work from home—legal writing. |
| 3:00 p.m. | Work from home—legal writing. |
| 4:00 p.m. | Check email. |
| 5:00 p.m. | Facebook Live show on Eagan Immigration Facebook page. Then, walk the dogs. |
| 6:00 p.m. | Go to the playground with the kid. |
| 7:00 p.m. | Dinner. |
| 8:00 p.m. | Kid in bed. Watch TV with husband. |
| 9:00 p.m. | Get ready for bed and read. |
| 10:00 p.m. | Lights out. |
| 11:00 p.m. | Sleep. |
| 12:00 a.m. | Sleep. |

## SAMPLE SCHEDULE—WEDNESDAY

| | |
|---|---|
| 5:00 a.m. | Wake up, make tea, do yoga. |
| 6:00 a.m. | Me time: read, work on non-firm projects, peruse social media, accomplish random tasks. |
| 7:00 a.m. | The kid wakes up, and morning routine: diaper, clothes, walk dogs while husband gets ready for work. |
| 8:00 a.m. | Send kid and husband off. Shower and get dressed. |
| 9:00 a.m. | FREEDOM!!! Enjoy a leisurely breakfast and listen to a book on Audible. |
| 10:00 a.m. | Hair appointment. |

*(continued)*

**SAMPLE SCHEDULE—WEDNESDAY** *(continued)*

| | |
|---|---|
| 11:00 a.m. | Hair appointment. |
| 12:00 p.m. | Go out to lunch. |
| 1:00 p.m. | Mani-pedi. |
| 2:00 p.m. | Mani-pedi. |
| 3:00 p.m. | Run errands. |
| 4:00 p.m. | Run errands. |
| 5:00 p.m. | Massage. |
| 6:00 p.m. | Head home. |
| 7:00 p.m. | Dinner. |
| 8:00 p.m. | Kid in bed. Watch TV with husband. |
| 9:00 p.m. | Get ready for bed and read. |
| 10:00 p.m. | Lights out. |
| 11:00 p.m. | Sleep. |
| 12:00 a.m. | Sleep. |

**SAMPLE SCHEDULE—SATURDAY**

| | |
|---|---|
| 5:00 a.m. | Wake up, make tea, do yoga. |
| 6:00 a.m. | Me time: read, work on non-firm projects, peruse social media, accomplish random tasks. |
| 7:00 a.m. | The kid wakes up. Morning snuggles, then make a family breakfast while husband takes care of the kid and walks the dogs. |
| 8:00 a.m. | Family breakfast, then get ready for work. |
| 9:00 a.m. | Leave for the office. |

**SAMPLE SCHEDULE—SATURDAY** *(continued)*

| | |
|---|---|
| 10:00 a.m. | Consultation or contract signing meeting. |
| 11:00 a.m. | Consultation or contract signing meeting. |
| 12:00 p.m. | Consultation or contract signing meeting. |
| 1:00 p.m. | Consultation or contract signing meeting. |
| 2:00 p.m. | Consultation or contract signing meeting. |
| 3:00 p.m. | Consultation or contract signing meeting. |
| 4:00 p.m. | Consultation or contract signing meeting. |
| 5:00 p.m. | Head home. |
| 6:00 p.m. | Family time. |
| 7:00 p.m. | Family time. |
| 8:00 p.m. | Kid in bed. Watch TV with husband. |
| 9:00 p.m. | Get ready for bed and read. |
| 10:00 p.m. | Lights out. |
| 11:00 p.m. | Sleep. |
| 12:00 a.m. | Sleep. |

This should give you an idea of what is possible, especially if you're really struggling to break free of the nine-to-five mind-set. I also want to note that your schedule can change as your life changes. You will see in my schedule that I am a bit more of a homebody now and enjoy spending time with my family. That's because I have a kid and am now in my mid-thirties. I don't want to go out every night. I want to run errands, spend time by myself, and play with my kid. But this schedule looked very different when I first started my firm. Keep that in mind as you grow and evolve. Your schedule can grow and evolve, too, and so can your law firm.

Now it's time for you to plan out your weeks. Refer back to your list of your nonwork priorities and incorporate them. As you do this exercise, if you think of other activities you want to add, do it! This is your life and your schedule. Your firm will work around it.

## MONDAY

| | |
|---|---|
| 5:00 a.m. | |
| 6:00 a.m. | |
| 7:00 a.m. | |
| 8:00 a.m. | |
| 9:00 a.m. | |
| 10:00 a.m. | |
| 11:00 a.m. | |
| 12:00 p.m. | |
| 1:00 p.m. | |
| 2:00 p.m. | |
| 3:00 p.m. | |
| 4:00 p.m. | |
| 5:00 p.m. | |
| 6:00 p.m. | |
| 7:00 p.m. | |
| 8:00 p.m. | |
| 9:00 p.m. | |
| 10:00 p.m. | |
| 11:00 p.m. | |
| 12:00 a.m. | |

**TUESDAY**

| | |
|---|---|
| 5:00 a.m. | |
| 6:00 a.m. | |
| 7:00 a.m. | |
| 8:00 a.m. | |
| 9:00 a.m. | |
| 10:00 a.m. | |
| 11:00 a.m. | |
| 12:00 p.m. | |
| 1:00 p.m. | |
| 2:00 p.m. | |
| 3:00 p.m. | |
| 4:00 p.m. | |
| 5:00 p.m. | |
| 6:00 p.m. | |
| 7:00 p.m. | |
| 8:00 p.m. | |
| 9:00 p.m. | |
| 10:00 p.m. | |
| 11:00 p.m. | |
| 12:00 a.m. | |

## WEDNESDAY

| | |
|---|---|
| 5:00 a.m. | |
| 6:00 a.m. | |
| 7:00 a.m. | |
| 8:00 a.m. | |
| 9:00 a.m. | |
| 10:00 a.m. | |
| 11:00 a.m. | |
| 12:00 p.m. | |
| 1:00 p.m. | |
| 2:00 p.m. | |
| 3:00 p.m. | |
| 4:00 p.m. | |
| 5:00 p.m. | |
| 6:00 p.m. | |
| 7:00 p.m. | |
| 8:00 p.m. | |
| 9:00 p.m. | |
| 10:00 p.m. | |
| 11:00 p.m. | |
| 12:00 a.m. | |

## THURSDAY

| | |
|---|---|
| 5:00 a.m. | |
| 6:00 a.m. | |
| 7:00 a.m. | |
| 8:00 a.m. | |
| 9:00 a.m. | |
| 10:00 a.m. | |
| 11:00 a.m. | |
| 12:00 p.m. | |
| 1:00 p.m. | |
| 2:00 p.m. | |
| 3:00 p.m. | |
| 4:00 p.m. | |
| 5:00 p.m. | |
| 6:00 p.m. | |
| 7:00 p.m. | |
| 8:00 p.m. | |
| 9:00 p.m. | |
| 10:00 p.m. | |
| 11:00 p.m. | |
| 12:00 a.m. | |

**FRIDAY**

| | |
|---|---|
| 5:00 a.m. | |
| 6:00 a.m. | |
| 7:00 a.m. | |
| 8:00 a.m. | |
| 9:00 a.m. | |
| 10:00 a.m. | |
| 11:00 a.m. | |
| 12:00 p.m. | |
| 1:00 p.m. | |
| 2:00 p.m. | |
| 3:00 p.m. | |
| 4:00 p.m. | |
| 5:00 p.m. | |
| 6:00 p.m. | |
| 7:00 p.m. | |
| 8:00 p.m. | |
| 9:00 p.m. | |
| 10:00 p.m. | |
| 11:00 p.m. | |
| 12:00 a.m. | |

## SATURDAY

| | |
|---|---|
| 5:00 a.m. | |
| 6:00 a.m. | |
| 7:00 a.m. | |
| 8:00 a.m. | |
| 9:00 a.m. | |
| 10:00 a.m. | |
| 11:00 a.m. | |
| 12:00 p.m. | |
| 1:00 p.m. | |
| 2:00 p.m. | |
| 3:00 p.m. | |
| 4:00 p.m. | |
| 5:00 p.m. | |
| 6:00 p.m. | |
| 7:00 p.m. | |
| 8:00 p.m. | |
| 9:00 p.m. | |
| 10:00 p.m. | |
| 11:00 p.m. | |
| 12:00 a.m. | |

## SUNDAY

| | |
|---|---|
| 5:00 a.m. | |
| 6:00 a.m. | |
| 7:00 a.m. | |
| 8:00 a.m. | |
| 9:00 a.m. | |
| 10:00 a.m. | |
| 11:00 a.m. | |
| 12:00 p.m. | |
| 1:00 p.m. | |
| 2:00 p.m. | |
| 3:00 p.m. | |
| 4:00 p.m. | |
| 5:00 p.m. | |
| 6:00 p.m. | |
| 7:00 p.m. | |
| 8:00 p.m. | |
| 9:00 p.m. | |
| 10:00 p.m. | |
| 11:00 p.m. | |
| 12:00 a.m. | |

How did that feel? Did you include time for all the things that are important to you outside of work? If you are worried about having enough time for work, don't! In the next section, you'll learn several efficiency tips so you can cut your work time way down and still get everything done.

Before we move on, put your new schedule somewhere you will see it often. If this is a different way of thinking for you, it will take some getting used to, and having a constant reminder will help you stay on track. So, rip those pages out of the book and hang them over your desk. Or turn them into a Google Doc that automatically pops up when you open your web browser. Or create calendar events. Do whatever necessary to keep this new schedule fresh in your mind and ensure you stick to it.

## PLAN YOUR VACATIONS

Another important element of healthy work-life balance is actually taking vacations. And when I say "vacation," I'm talking about a complete break from work, not a trip that you spend in your hotel room checking emails and drafting legal briefs. An actual vacation. I have observed that for many law firm owners, the idea of taking a vacation and completely leaving the firm for a period of time is terrifying. They can't imagine the firm will survive their absence, and as a result, many firm owners go years without taking a break. This is terrible for mental health, productivity, and efficiency.

To avoid procrastinating on vacations and mental health breaks, you need to plan in advance. If you're in a serious relationship and will vacation with your significant other, you can do this section together. Figure out what you want and take concrete steps toward making the vacation a reality, such as purchasing flights.

In this section, you will do some vacation planning. Start by determining how much time you want to spend away from the firm each year. A minimum of two weeks is good to really clear your head. Then, decide how you will allocate that vacation time. Will you take one long break, or will you take multiple, shorter breaks?

1. I will take __________ weeks of vacation each year.
2. I will divide that vacation time over __________ different vacations.

Next, think about what you want your vacations to look like. You can take trips to new places, you can visit family, or you can plan a staycation, where you don't even leave the area, but simply take time to yourself away from work. Whatever you choose, create a plan to truly disconnect. List a few ideas for your vacations for the upcoming year:

1. ______________________________________________
2. ______________________________________________
3. ______________________________________________
4. ______________________________________________
5. ______________________________________________

Now, take some steps to ensure you actually take the vacations you planned. Talk to your significant other and select specific dates. Add those dates to the calendar. Start looking into any flights, hotels, or other travel planning you need to accomplish.

Even though you worked out a good weekly schedule, it is important for you to truly disconnect from your law firm once in a while. This may seem impossible, especially when you're broke and just getting started, but that's when it's even more important. Get into the habit now of taking time for yourself, and stick with it. As your firm grows and becomes busier and busier, it is incredibly important for your sanity that you regularly take time away to clear your mind, refocus, and come back refreshed and energized.

## BECOME INCREDIBLY EFFICIENT

In order to enjoy a flexible workweek and take your much-needed vacations, you must learn to by hyperefficient. Now that you have your own business, any time you waste during the workday just takes away from time for yourself and time you could spend on tasks that actually make your firm money.

In this section, I will teach you my favorite efficiency techniques. Use them, and you will instantly create a ton of extra time for yourself, while still getting everything checked off your to-do list.

### Communication

The various forms of communication are huge time sucks in most businesses, and law firms are no different. People waste time emailing, perusing social media, and even just popping into each other's offices to chat. Throughout the day, all these different communications add up to hours of wasted time.

The quickest way to create lots of time in your schedule is to eliminate random communication throughout the day. We'll go through each form of communication to show you exactly how to do this.

#### *Email*

Email is the biggest time sucker in a business. Most people check their email constantly throughout the day, responding as soon as something hits their inbox. However, this dramatically reduces efficiency and wastes tons of time.

Let's look at an example:

> You wake up in the morning, intending to work on a particular case all day and get it filed. Nothing will distract you! But as soon as you start work, you check your email. There are several emails in your inbox, and you respond to them all. Some require additional research, time spent looking for documents to attach, or a review of your calendar. You finish about 45 minutes later.
>
> Then you start working on your case. As you are working, you notice an email notification in your inbox. You switch over to your email, read the email, take a

quick look at your calendar to respond, and then respond. This takes about five minutes. Then you go back to working on the case. You have to pause to remember exactly where you left off and get your train of thought back on track.

This goes on regularly throughout the day, at least once every half hour. By the end of the day, you've wasted over an hour checking your email, not including all the times you spent losing your train of thought on your casework. You're so close to finishing prepping that case, but you're not quite there. And you still have more email to respond to. You wrap up and plan to finish it tomorrow.

Now imagine a scenario in which you respond to the same emails, work on the same case, and do all of it in half the time. This is completely possible by blocking your time. Instead of checking your email throughout the day, select two times each day when you pause the work you are doing, check and respond to email, and then resume your work. Aside from those two times each day, keep your email closed and notifications off.

Using this blocking method, you can efficiently power through all of your emails, without the constant distraction throughout the day. This will allow you to focus on your other tasks completely and still ensures each email receives a timely response.

When selecting the times to check your email each day, select the first time slot for two to three hours after you start your day, so you can get a couple focused work hours in before the distraction of random emails. Then, select a second time toward the end of your workday so you can respond to any remaining emails before you leave the office.

I like to check my email at noon and 4:00 p.m. I find that if I don't check my email before noon, I can get in a few good hours of work with no distractions. Plus, if I'm trying to be extra efficient, I can respond to them while I eat my lunch. The 4:00 p.m. slot ensures that I've gone through emails sent later in the day before finishing work but still allows me to wrap up by 4:30 or so.

Select two times you will check your email each day:

1. ____________________

2. ____________________

This is going to be a big change, so it may be hard to stick to. But if you do, you will notice a significant increase in your productivity, and you will probably finish your tasks much earlier than normal. After I implemented this simple trick, I was able to take regular half days and actually accomplished more than I did working a full day. Without email constantly distracting me from my tasks throughout the day, I became much more efficient and accomplished tasks quickly. You will do the same.

### *Social Media*

Oh, man, social media. The king of all time sucks. Raise your hand if you've checked some sort of social media in the last hour. How about the last 10 minutes? Social media is incredibly addictive, and it's hard to refrain from constantly checking for new likes, shares, or updates. This one is extra tricky because many law firms, mine included, rely on social media for advertising and interacting with and learning from other attorneys. Which means there's always an easy excuse to hop on "for work."

Even if you use social media for work, you have to be strategic about it. It's not helpful to your work if social media becomes a distraction from the actual tasks you need to focus on and allows you to waste time you could spend on other, more important things. Just as with email, every time you check social media, you lose focus on your current task and break your train of thought. And, even worse than with email, it is so easy to get lost perusing social media. You can check the clock and see that an hour has passed, and you didn't do anything except scroll through your feed.

There are a few different ways to reduce your social media use. The first is to do the same thing as email and set specific times each day when you are allowed to use social media. If you go with this option, consider checking social media right after you finish with your email. That way, you aren't taking additional, distracting breaks from your real work.

Another option is to eliminate or limit your time on social media each day. I like this option because it ensures you know exactly how much time you will waste on social media and prevents you from an endless binge. If you go with this option, I highly suggest you use an app or a Web extension, such as StayFocusd for Google Chrome, that restricts the time you spend on certain websites.

I used StayFocusd and it really helps me—drumroll, please—stay focused throughout the day. I have it set to apply to the hours from 9:00 a.m. to 4:00 p.m. Monday through Friday, and I only allow myself 30 minutes on my restricted websites during that window. On my restricted websites list, I've added all social media, all my email accounts, and all the other random websites I use as procrastination tools, such as Amazon, my bank account, Rent the Runway, and Etsy.[1]

A final option is to completely cut the cord on social media. This might not be a bad idea if you are really addicted. Think of it like a juice cleanse. You take a few days or weeks to detox, and then you slowly reintroduce various food groups or, in this case, social media platforms.

I previously mentioned that I use StayFocusd on Google Chrome, but I found I was cheating by checking social media on my phone. So, I ended up wiping all social media off my phone for a time. It was amazing! Excruciating, terrible, chill-inducing, but amazing. I had so much free time! The first couple weeks I constantly reached for my phone out of habit. Stop at a red light, reach for phone. Hop out of the shower, reach for phone. Bored on a conference call, reach for phone. After a while, though, my body started to remember that there were no longer any interesting apps on my phone, and the addiction went away. If this is you and you totally wipe your phone, know that you will get past the addiction. And I'm not being facetious here. Social media can become an addiction.

---

[1] Yes, I'm basic, and I'm okay with that. I thought about lying and writing things like "the *Washington Post*," and "the *Economist*," but I just couldn't do it.

After you get the addiction out of your system, you can add apps back onto your phone. But take it slow. Some platforms may just be too addictive for you and will always ruin your productivity. Avoid those. Pay attention to your reactions to each app and tread carefully. Social media is not worth the effect on your productivity and your business.

Use the following checklist to decide exactly how you will reduce your social media use. Remember, you can try something for a bit, and if you find it's not working, switch tactics.

To reduce my social media use, I will:

- Check social media at these specific times each day: ____________________________.
- Limit social media use to ____________ minutes each day.
- Use this specific app to stay accountable: ______________________.
- Wipe all social media apps from phone.
- Deactivate social media accounts.

### Phone Calls

Constant phone calls, either incoming or outgoing, throughout the day will create major distractions as you try to accomplish actual work. Managing phone calls can be tricky because you must be available for clients, other attorneys, and other business contacts, but you cannot allow calls to stifle your productivity. This section includes a few different tactics for reducing the time you waste on phone calls.

This first technique works well for attorneys who have a receptionist, whether it is someone on staff or someone who answers phones through the firm's virtual office space. When using a receptionist, have him or her answer all calls. Tell the receptionist not to forward any calls to you no matter what. If "no matter what" is too extreme, give your receptionist very limited circumstances in which he or she can forward calls, but "it's an emergency" should not be one. To clients, everything is an emergency. An example from my own practice is that my receptionist can forward any calls from the court.

Then ask your receptionist to take detailed messages for you, but to hold the messages until your designated "communication time"—preferably at the same time you check your email. Have your receptionist send you all the messages at that specific time so you can address them in bulk. This protects you from constant interruptions as messages come in, as well as the internal struggle between continuing your work and pausing to return the call. Plus, if you have a specific time set aside to return calls, your receptionist can tell clients to expect a call back around that time. Knowing the specific time you will call back further encourages clients to leave a message without too much complaint.

The next option is modified for those who do not have a receptionist. Under this model, you can leave a message in your outgoing voice mail. Try something like: "You have reached [Name of law firm]. Please leave your name, number, and a brief message, and I will return your call at either 12:00 p.m. or 4:00 p.m. today or the next business day." Keeping the message brief ensures clients are likely to listen to it and leave a message.

Setting client expectations is helpful here. When someone hires you, it's a good idea to say something like, "I spend a lot of time in court and in meetings, which means

I won't always answer the phone. However, I typically return all calls at 12:00 p.m. and 4:00 p.m. same day or the next business day, if you leave a message, I will get back to you." That way, your clients know from the beginning that you do not constantly monitor your phone and will not freak out if you don't answer.

If you are building your client base and are worried about missing potential clients who do not leave a message, just return all the missed calls during your communication time, even if the caller did not leave a message. This ensures that you're touching base with everyone who calls, and it shows potential clients that you take their calls seriously.

### *Office Hours*

The final time suck is in-office chitchat. If you are solo and using a virtual office and you work from home most of the time, this may not apply. But read it anyway because you might have a staff someday.

The best way to avoid office chitchat is to have a closed-door policy with specific open-door office hours. Again, set your office hours during your "communication time" when you go through email, check social media, and respond to calls. Having specific office hours has multiple benefits. First, it allows you to focus during the rest of the day. And second, it forces staff to figure things out on their own, instead of coming to you for every little question.

If you have a staff that is used to asking you questions throughout the day, explain this new policy and the reasons behind it. Make sure they understand it is strictly about your productivity and not about them. You may also need to actually lock your door and ignore knocking during your closed-door policy. Staff will forget, and it will be tempting to help them. Be really strict with yourself and with them, especially in the beginning, as you all form a new habit. If you're really struggling, but a big stop sign on your door—that way you see it every time you are tempted to open up.

Another option is to have a primarily virtual law firm. This means you and your staff work remotely most of the time and are only required to come into the office for client meetings and staff meetings and to get things filed. This works really well if you have a team you can trust to work on their own. If you have a self-motivated team and can let go of control, it is an amazing way to increase efficiency. If everyone is working remotely, they will not be tempted to waste time chatting or asking you questions. Which means you can work in efficient peace and quiet all day.

Regardless of the option you choose, you must find a way to reduce time wasted chatting. All of these little conversations add up to a lot over the course of a day and dig into your personal time outside of the office.

## Work Product

The next step on your path to hyperefficiency is to create templates for everything. I mean, EVERYTHING. From your retainer agreement, to client welcome letters, to briefs, to checklists. Everybody in your firm (even if it's just you) should be working from templates 90 percent of the time.

When it comes to drafting legal work and communicating with clients, most of what we spend our energy and brainpower on is creating original work. This includes researching specific issues, drafting creative arguments, writing letters to clients, and so much more. If you can eliminate the majority of this original work by creating templates for almost everything you do, you will save hours and hours of time each week.

When you begin the task of creating templates, keep it simple. Unless you are already really savvy at the macro and other template functions in Word, Google Docs, or another program, no need for fancy templates that autofill. If you really want templates like that, you can update your initial templates once you learn more or hire someone to help. For now, the goal is just to create the templates, so stick to the basics.

Start by using a work product you have already created to make templates. For example, do you have a retainer agreement you used with a prior client? Turn it into a template. If there are sections that frequently change, such as the name of the client or the matter, make sure they are easy to find. Use brackets for all language that needs to change, such as "[Client Name]," but highlighting those areas works just as well. You can even create a separate document for matter templates that you can quickly add into your retainer agreement depending on the matter or case type.

For complicated legal work, such as briefs, the task of creating a template may seem impossible. It's not. Think about a legal brief, for example. Typically, we write our briefs in ILAC format: Introduction, Law, Analysis, Conclusion. For the introduction, there is a lot of language that repeats in each case. That language can be templated, and then the case-specific details, such as the facts and procedural history, can get filled in on a case-by-case basis. As for the law, there will be a lot of overlap across different but similar cases. Create a separate document that just includes the relevant sections of the law, divided up by legal issues. That way, you can just grab the law that applies and quickly add it to your brief, depending on the issue at hand. Your analysis section will require the most original thinking, but there are still probably some areas that you repeat, brief after brief. Keep those in, and then delineate the areas you will need to fill in with case-specific details. Finally, conclusions often include similar language for similar cases. Template as much as you can and then change the details for each case.

See, that wasn't too bad. There will always be some details you need to update in your template, but the idea is to reuse as much as possible. This will save you a ton of time from case to case, and it will also provide clear guidelines for staff now or in the future.

Now, create a list of all the things you will template. Here is a list to get you started, but remember, every practice area is different, so you will need to fill in a lot yourself:

- ❐ Retainer agreement
    - ❐ Retainer agreement matters
- ❐ Welcome letter, by case type
- ❐ Closing letter, by case type

- ❐ Client document checklist, by case type
- ❐ Client questionnaire, by case type
- ❐ Fax cover letter
- ❐ Routine emails
- ❐ Brief or cover letter, by case type
- ❐ Internal checklists, by case type
- ❐ Invoice
- ❐ Receipt
- ❐ Motions, different types
- ❐ ______________________________
- ❐ ______________________________
- ❐ ______________________________
- ❐ ______________________________
- ❐ ______________________________

For work product you have not created yet but know you will want to template, just turn your first version into a template. If you have extra time on your hands, create a template from scratch right now, but if you don't have time for that, just wait until you create an original version of that document, and turn it into a template. Do this for all original work.

## Setting Tasks

Another must-do for becoming more efficient and spending less time in the office is to set daily tasks for yourself and stick to them. The first rule of task-setting is to set your tasks for the day at least one day in advance—you are not allowed to assign yourself tasks the same day they are due. This forces you to look at the big picture and set tasks based on what truly needs to get done the next day. If you allow yourself to set tasks on the day they are due, you will begin adding small, less-important tasks throughout the day that will clutter your schedule and make you less productive. Unless a task is a true emergency, set it for another day.

Along those lines, it can be very helpful to accomplish tasks in bulk. For example, perhaps you spend Mondays working on administrative tasks for the firm. And maybe on Tuesdays, you crank out a ton of legal work. Bulking similar tasks together helps you stay focused and in the zone, rather than constantly switching things up.

Next, assign yourself only three to four tasks per day. This is a reasonable amount to ensure you are allowing yourself enough time to accomplish each task without overwhelming yourself. Three to four tasks doesn't sound like many when you first start, but when you accomplish this many tasks each day, you will find yourself moving through your tasks quickly and efficiently.

Review all your cases weekly and assign tasks for the upcoming week. I typically review all my cases on Monday morning, assigning myself tasks through the end of the week. This allows me to work around a fairly up-to-date calendar, ensures I am staying on top of all my cases, and assigns my tasks at one time, instead of throughout the week. By bulking the assignment of tasks into one day, I save myself time throughout the week.

Use this weekly task list to fill in your tasks for this week. You can also use the template in Appendix A or download a fillable template at https://ambar.org/startalawfirm.

## WEEKLY TASKS

| | |
|---|---|
| Monday | •<br>•<br>•<br>• |
| Tuesday | •<br>•<br>•<br>• |
| Wednesday | •<br>•<br>•<br>• |
| Thursday | •<br>•<br>•<br>• |
| Friday | •<br>•<br>•<br>• |
| Saturday | •<br>•<br>•<br>• |
| Sunday | •<br>•<br>•<br>• |

Finally, when you finish your tasks, stop working! This will be hard for many of you workaholics, and you may initially feel guilty about wrapping up your day early. It may also be hard for others in your life to swallow, especially those with a nine-to-five job. However, it's time for you to shift your mind-set a bit. If you have accomplished all of your tasks for the day, why sit around waiting for five o'clock to go out and enjoy your life? Isn't this why you started your own law firm? To have the flexibility to come and go as you please? To make money on your terms? Find yourself a hobby, and once you've finished your tasks, go enjoy it.

## Don't Let Things Pile Up

Staying organized will keep your firm running smoothly and you working efficiently, but that is easier said than done when running your own firm. It seems impossible to remember all the administrative tasks, marketing tasks, accounting tasks, HR tasks, and so many others, on top of the tasks and deadlines for your cases. No wonder firm owners never seem to stop working.

To prevent this feeling of overwhelm in managing your firm, make a list of recurring tasks for your firm, and set a time each day, week, or month to accomplish those tasks. For example, if you are trying to increase your firm's social media presence, maybe a daily task is to post something on your firm's Facebook page. Or, from an accounting perspective, perhaps you send out invoices to all your clients every month. These are just two examples of recurring tasks you will be responsible for in your firm. Having a clear checklist to refer to daily, weekly, and monthly will ensure you stay on track with everything you have to accomplish.

I have included an example of what I use for my firm in Appendix B. Keeping everything organized from the beginning will ensure you don't waste time putting out fires down the road. It will also help you work more quickly and efficiently so you can get through your tasks faster and out enjoying life sooner.

### CHAPTER CHECKLIST: GET FOCUSED AND EFFICIENT

- ❒ **Create your ideal week.** Figure out what you want your workweek to look like. Get out of the nine-to-five mind-set.
- ❒ **Plan vacations.** Get vacations on the calendar NOW, even if they are just staycations away from work. Take concrete steps to planning your vacations.
- ❒ **Schedule specific times to check email.** Then shut down your email and do not open it except at those specific times.
- ❒ **Get your social media use under control.** Select specific times to check social media. Use a website blocker. Wipe social media from your phone. Whichever option(s) you choose, control your social media habit.

- ❒ **Schedule time to return phone calls.** Select times. Train your receptionist on taking messages and how to respond to calls. Set up your voice mail message.
- ❒ **Schedule office hours.** Train your staff on your new office hours policy. Stick to it.
- ❒ **Create templates.** For work you have already created, turn it into a template. For work you have not created yet, either create a template from scratch, or create a template the first time you create the work product.
- ❒ **Set tasks.** Set a handful of tasks at least one day in advance. Do not change your tasks day of. Stop working when you complete your tasks for the day.
- ❒ **Create routine task lists.** Create daily, weekly, monthly, and annual checklists to ensure things do not slip through the cracks.

CHAPTER 8

# Outsourcing and Delegating

**OUTLINE**



If you've reached a point in your business where you need help and can afford it, congratulations! This is a very exciting step for your firm, and it's important to navigate it carefully to ensure your business continues to grow and thrive. Hire too fast, and you might not be able to pay your employees. Hire too slow, and you might start seeing the scales of work–life balance tip until you come crashing down. Fortunately, there are ways to begin outsourcing your tasks that will allow you to continue increasing your profit while decreasing your stress.

## HOW TO KNOW WHEN YOU'RE READY TO GROW

The two main things you need to look at when deciding whether you're ready to hire help are your workload and your profit margin. If you decide to hire someone to assist you in your business, you must ensure you have enough work for that person and enough money to pay him or her.

### Work

Determining whether you have enough work for another person entails more than just feeling like you cannot accomplish everything by yourself. This is the first step, but you must determine how much overflow work you actually have. Is it enough to sustain an employee? For how many hours per week?

Make a list of all the tasks you work on in a given month. Determine how many hours per month you spend on each task. Once you've created a list of all the tasks in your business, go through and determine which tasks you could delegate. Aside from purely legal work, which other tasks must you and only you handle at this stage in your practice? Anything else can be delegated.

Of the tasks you can delegate, determine who can accomplish those tasks for you. For example, a legal assistant might be able to handle answering the phone and filling out forms with clients, but you will need an accountant to handle your taxes. Dividing up your tasks this way will help you determine who you need to hire and what your hiring priorities are.

### Money

Now we need to determine if you have enough money to hire someone, even part-time, to handle some of the tasks you identified. To do that, we will use some simple math. This should be easy if you've been keeping track of your finances, as instructed earlier in the book.

Determine your average monthly revenue for your business (income only). Now, subtract all your monthly business expenses, as well as your necessary personal expenses. This leaves you with the amount of money you have leftover for any extras, such as an employee.

Now that we've looked at the tasks you can delegate, as well as the money you can afford to pay someone to help with those tasks, we need to determine if it will work. This is where you need to determine what type of position you want to fill and do a little research in your market. Just to get a general idea, look on Craigslist or Indeed to determine general wages offered. Also talk to colleagues with staff to see what they suggest paying.

Once you've established the position you want to hire, how much work you have to give someone in that position, and how much money you have available to pay an employee, do a little math to figure out if it will all work. Make sure to add about 10 percent to cover additional taxes for an employee, plus the cost of any extra expenses, such as a computer for your employee. And remember, you don't need to hire someone full-time, nor do you need to begin with a paid position; offering an internship might be a workable solution at the start. You can start as your budget allows, and then grow the position as your firm grows.

## HOW TO GROW SLOWLY AND CAREFULLY

Whether or not you have the budget to hire somebody, there are various different options for getting the help you need as your firm grows. When it comes to money, it's best to start out conservatively and then increase wages or hours once you're sure the budget allows.

For those who have a low budget or who are new to hiring and managing, start with an intern. The local law schools are often teeming with law students searching for an internship, and many will work for free. This is a great way for both the law student to get some experience and for you to get some help. And who knows, maybe you will end up with a law student who is such a great fit with your firm that you'll ultimately hire him or her for an associate position in the future. That's what happened to me, and my associate could not be a better fit.

If you're looking for something more permanent but still have a low budget, try hiring someone on a part-time, contract basis. The benefit of contract employees is that they use their own equipment, and you are not responsible for paying taxes as an employer. Additionally, contract employees are typically very flexible, so you can give them a lot of work when you are really busy and then taper off when things slow down.

However, if you hire a contract attorney, make sure the position is truly a contract position. Check the guidelines in your state, as some states define a contractor much more narrowly than others. Usually individuals who are self-employed and work for various other companies fall squarely into the category of contractors, but you should still double-check.

If you are looking for someone to help answer the phones, a fairly inexpensive option is to contract a virtual answering service. This is much less expensive than a full-time receptionist, and these companies often offer service 24/7. A Google search for "phone answering service" yields a lot of different results, including Ruby Receptionists, which some of my colleagues recommend.

Finally, if you've decided you want an actual employee to work with you either in the office or virtually, go for it! If you have the funds to pay the employee, in addition to taxes, any benefits, and the additional office expenses, it is a great next step. If you can afford it but are still nervous, start your new employee on a part-time basis. When I hired my legal assistant, I told him he would start at 10 to 20 hours per week. After about a month, his assistance was so beneficial to the firm that he became a full-time employee. However, I needed to take baby steps to reach that point.

## TIPS FOR HIRING

When I hired my first employee, I was incredibly nervous. Hiring staff is a big step for a business, especially when you started broke. On top of that, I knew I wanted my employee to work virtually most of the time, so I had to find someone reliable.

Over the years, after lots of trial and error and bouncing ideas around with colleagues, I developed a good strategy for hiring. If you follow this straightforward process, step-by-step, you will greatly increase the odds of finding the right employee for your firm.

1. **Look online.** Post an ad on Craigslist, Indeed, or another site that caters to your potential employee.
2. **Be specific.** In the post, make very specific requests. I always request a cover letter in English and Spanish (Spanish fluency is a job requirement in my firm), a résumé,

and three references. Toward the end of the post, I always write, "Please reply with EI02072019 in the subject line."

These very specific requirements are designed to help me quickly see who has good attention to detail and follows instructions. If I get an application that doesn't meet these requirements, it goes straight into the trash.

3. **Start with a phone interview.** Never waste your time starting with an in-person interview. Do a phone interview first, and ask the applicant to call you. That way, you can see if they are on time with their phone call.

   Then start your initial questioning. Go through their résumé and dig into their specific experience. Try to get a sense of whether they have the right experience and would be a good fit for the position. This call usually lasts 15 to 30 minutes.
4. **Send a follow-up task.** After the phone interview, send the applicant a follow-up task. It should be fairly straightforward and related to the position—usually I give them a hypothetical set of facts and a short form to fill out. Don't give them a deadline to complete it.

   Sending the follow-up task allows you to see the applicant's attention to detail in completing the task, and by not assigning a due date, you will learn what the applicant considers a reasonable response time for that level of work. If the work is not completed well or is completed too slowly, you will know to move on from that applicant.
5. **Call past employers.** Honestly, calling references gets you nowhere. Job candidates only select references who will give them a glowing recommendation, so you already know what you will get before you call.

   To get real answers, call the applicant's past employers. For current employers, ask permission first, as the individual may be job hunting on the sly. However, for past jobs where the applicant no longer works, do a little research to get the contact info, and pick up the phone.

   If the applicant worked at large companies and you need to get the contact information for a specific supervisor, talk to the applicant about it. Let him or her know you want to talk to the past supervisor and ask for a name. Before you make the call, ask the applicant what he or she thinks the supervisor will say. This is when you start to get some honest answers.
6. **Hold an in-person interview.** If the applicant has made it this far, do an in-person interview. Here you really get to the nitty-gritty of the applicant's experience and personality, and find out how he or she can benefit your firm. Take detailed notes during the interview process.

   There are lots of good books on the interview process, but check out *Who: The A Method for Hiring*, by Geoff Smart and Randy Street. It's a little intense, so you can tone it down to fit your needs, but it has some really great info.
7. **Make a decision.** At this stage, you should make a decision. It's okay if your decision is to bring the applicant in for another interview. It's also okay if your decision is to wait for somebody better to apply. It doesn't matter what you decide; you just need to decide *something*—for your own sanity, as well as that of the applicant.

Use these tips, and you will not regret it. By carefully following these guidelines, I was able to weed out applicants who had a poor attention to detail and ultimately found my amazing legal assistant. I hope he never leaves, and I hope you find an employee who is just as good!

## TRAIN 'EM UP AND KEEP 'EM HAPPY

Once you start hiring employees, you must train them and ensure they do the best work possible for your law firm. If they are good employees, make sure they continue to feel happy, motivated, and appreciated. It's much more cost-effective to keep a hard-working, happy employee than to rehire over and over again. Invest in your staff, and you will see the rewards from your investment.

### Nondisclosure

First things first, ethics. There are so many ethical rules associated with being a lawyer, but one of the most important ones is attorney–client privilege. Of course, you can share privileged information with your staff, but you must ensure they understand the importance of keeping that information confidential.

When you first hire staff members or contract workers, have them sign a nondisclosure agreement that explains attorney–client privilege and outlines the rules they must follow. Get this signed document back before you assign them any work.

Even after your employees start working, you should constantly keep an eye on any potential violations of attorney–client privilege. If you notice anything troubling, talk to your employee and explain how his or her actions could be violating attorney–client privilege. For nonattorneys, this is a foreign concept and sometimes takes a while to get used to. It's easy to want to vent to our friends about a case or to give a referral source an update on the case she referred. You, as the attorney, are ultimately responsible for any breach in attorney–client privilege and must make sure you are teaching your staff how to maintain it.

### Training Manual

As you start hiring employees, you should begin developing a training manual that outlines the procedures in your firm. In fact, even if you are only thinking of hiring employees, you should begin working on this manual. Writing a training manual can be quite an undertaking, but working on it little by little makes the task more manageable.

The goal of your training manual should be to create streamlined processes for your staff members to follow. This will make the transition easier as staff members leave and new staff members join. As things change in your firm, you will constantly update your training manual. I make a note of something I want to add or change to my firm's manual almost every day. It is a fluid document, but one that all your employees should have access to and use as a guide.

## Motivation and Bonuses

Even though you're broke, you need to find creative ways to keep your employees motivated and happy. The happier your staff is, the harder they will work for you. And if you make them feel supported and appreciated, they will become the driving force behind your business's success.

If you don't have the budget to increase your employees' salaries or give them expensive perks, think of other ways to make them feel appreciated. I like to give my staff small bonuses, such as $50, when I notice them really stepping up to the plate. These bonuses are unscheduled, but I always make it a point to tell the employee the specific reason why I am giving the bonus, emphasizing my appreciation for their work. My employees are always excited to receive these mini-bonuses, and I immediately see increased motivation.

Another idea is to plan a fun activity for your staff. My legal assistant loves soccer, so I bought him and his girlfriend tickets to a DC United soccer game. This did not cost too much, but it was fun for him and showed him I appreciate him and pay attention to his interests.

Finally, create motivating games. This one might be my favorite motivational tool, because almost everybody gets a little competitive and increases performance. Shortly after my Facebook marketing took off and I was starting to get a lot of calls, I wanted to focus on converting those calls into prepaid consultations. So, I told my legal assistant that each week he managed to get five prepaid consultations set up, I would give him a $50 bonus, plus $10 for each prepaid consultation after the initial five. Of all my motivational tools, this one yielded immediate results. For the following three to four weeks after my offer, he booked at least five prepaid consultations each week. To this day, he still averages about three weeks per month with five prepaid consultations. As I later told him, bribery works wonders!

There are many different ways to motivate and reward your employees. The most important thing is to consistently tell them they are appreciated, say thank you, and give specific examples of good work they have done. Sprinkle in little prizes, bonuses, and gifts now and then, and you will have employees who want to stay with you for the long haul. As your firm grows and you hire more staff, make employee appreciation and motivation a priority. You may run the firm, but they still help you succeed.

### CHAPTER CHECKLIST: GET HELP

- ❒ **Determine whether you're ready to hire.** Look at your workload and your bank account. Do you have enough overflow work to keep someone busy for at least a part-time position? Do you have enough monthly revenue or savings to pay for a new hire? If yes to both, you're ready.

- ❐ **Decide on the position you need to fill.** Look at the areas where you waste the most time. Can you delegate those tasks to someone else? If so, what job position do those tasks fall under? That's the position you need to fill.
- ❐ **Prepare a training manual.** Do this before you actually hire someone. Write down the process for completing every task this new hire will handle. Be detailed. Eventually, you will beef this up to include every task in the firm, so anyone coming on can immediately jump in and work.
- ❐ **Start the search.** Post the job. Depending on the position, you might post at law schools, on Craigslist, on Indeed, or on another online site.
- ❐ **Go through the interview process.** Do a phone interview, send a homework assignment, and then do one or more in-person interviews. With the applicant's permission, call past employers to get their feedback.
- ❐ **Hire.** Once you've found someone you think is the right fit for the job, make an offer.
- ❐ **Train your new hire.** If you want your new hire to succeed, you need to take the time to train him or her. Use your training manual, but also work one-on-one with the new hire to make sure he or she is grasping the concepts.
- ❐ **Create a motivation plan.** To keep your employee(s) motivated, develop goals and rewards that they can work toward. These can be sporadic or consistent. Whatever works for you and them.

CHAPTER 9

# Create a Business Plan

**OUTLINE**



Now that you have set up every aspect of your firm, determined your target client, and begun thinking about hiring staff, you must memorialize everything in a business plan. This is a fluid document, something you update regularly and use to stay focused on your goals. Your business plan is the document that truly converts you from just a boring old attorney to a hyperfocused, uber-responsible, super-intelligent business owner.

I must admit, very few small law firm owners I know have a business plan. Most of them just wing it, hoping to bring in enough business to meet their expenses. They are stressed, overwhelmed, and somewhat disconnected from the realities of their business. This is not what I want for you. I want you to be organized, understand the ins and outs of your business, know how you generate money, and feel in control.

At the inception of your business, you must create a business plan. It seems tedious and oftentimes redundant, but this business plan will guide your firm, keeping you on track and helping you make good business decisions. This, in turn, will help you make good money. The following sections will detail the basic areas you should include in your business plan. There will be questions addressed in each section, and you will find a template business plan you can use as you create your own.

## SECTION 1: EXECUTIVE SUMMARY

The executive summary is the most important part of your business plan. It is a summary of your business plan that gives a concise overview of how your business will work and is the section of your business plan that you can easily review for an overview of your firm as it currently is, as well as the firm's goals.

You should write the executive summary after you have prepared all the other sections of the business plan. For that reason, I will not address the executive summary right here, but will walk you through it at the end of this chapter after you have completed the other sections of your business plan.

## SECTION 2: BASIC BUSINESS CONCEPT

In the Basic Business Concept section of your business plan, you will outline your practice concept as you see it now. You will identify the types of cases you will handle, the clients you will serve, the type of work you will do, your overall marketing strategy, your firm's location, and the things that make your firm unique.

The basic business concept will include a thorough introduction, which should cover who your firm will serve, how you will serve this client base, and why you will be successful. It should then include a discussion of your marketing plan and how you will obtain new clients. Finally, you should outline the competitive advantages your firm offers. This introduction should serve as a detailed overview of your practice, setting up the next few sections of your business plan.

After your introduction, include a Definition of Practice subsection, which essentially outlines the basic information about your firm, including the legal name, founding date, legal form (we will talk about these in a later section of the book), state of establishment, owner, principal attorney, location, geographic area served, immediate goals, and progress of current goals. I prepared this section more in bullet-point form in my business plan, but the style is up to you.

Finally, include a Practice Area subsection, where you go into detail about your practice area, the types of cases you will take, and the need for such services.

The following is a template you can fill in, with questions to guide you through some areas. Think carefully about the different aspects of your firm, and then begin filling everything in. Right now, just take notes and actively brainstorm. Once you've gone through this entire section of the chapter, download the editable blank template, also available in Appendix F, and use it to create your official business plan.

### BUSINESS PLAN: BASIC BUSINESS CONCEPT

| | |
|---|---|
| **Introduction**<br>Is there a need for your services in the area? Why?<br>Who will you serve?<br>What types of cases will you handle?<br>How will you develop new business?<br>What are your competitive advantages compared to other law firms in the area? | |

**BUSINESS PLAN: BASIC BUSINESS CONCEPT** *(continued)*

| Definition of Practice | Firm name:<br>Founding date:<br>Legal form:<br>State of establishment:<br>Owner:<br>Principal attorney:<br>Location:<br>Geographic area served:<br>Immediate goals:<br>Progress of current goals: |
|---|---|
| Practice Area<br>What is your overarching practice area?<br>What specific subsets of that practice area does your firm handle?<br>Why is there a need for assistance in those areas? | |

Hopefully you were able to easily fill out this template after having worked through some of the previous chapters. If not, this is a good opportunity to really think about your practice, your goals, and your client base. If you weren't sure how to fill in these sections right away, that's fine. Just grab some scratch paper or a computer and really think about your practice. Take notes and even talk to others if you need to. When you have a clear idea of how to fill in these sections of your business plan, come back to the book and jot down your ideas in the template.

# SECTION 3: MARKET ANALYSIS

The next step of your business plan is to do a market analysis and address your findings in your business plan. The Market Analysis section is comprised of two main parts: your target market and your competitive analysis. We will go through both subsections individually before adding the information to the Market Analysis template.

## Target Market

We discussed your target market earlier in the book. In that section, you should have filled out the Ideal Client Worksheet and summarized your ideal client. Write that summary here, so you can quickly reference it when it's time to add it to the business plan:

______________________________________________________________

______________________________________________________________

______________________________________________________________.

This is a good refresher, but make sure to add as much detail about your target client to your business plan as possible. The more detailed you are, the better you can focus your marketing and goals.

## Competitive Analysis

For this subsection of your business plan, you must do a little outside research. Look up your competitors and compare yourself to them. Start by finding other law firms in the same geographic location that cater to a similar client base. Go to their websites and evaluate their strengths, weaknesses, and the thing that makes them stand out from other firms. Jot down some notes in the following worksheet.

### ANALYSIS OF THE COMPETITION

| Firm Name | Strengths | Weaknesses | Special Qualities |
|---|---|---|---|
| | | | |
| | | | |
| | | | |
| | | | |
| | | | |
| | | | |

Now that you've looked into a few other competing firms in the area, make the same analysis for yourself. What are your strengths? How can you improve? What special qualities does your firm offer that other firms do not? Fill out your thoughts in the following worksheet.

## ANALYSIS OF YOUR BUSINESS

| Strengths | Weaknesses | Special Qualities |
|---|---|---|
| | | |
| | | |

At this point you have analyzed your target market, as well as the competition. With the information you gathered and jotted down in the previous few worksheets, start filling in the Market Analysis section of your business plan. Next is a Market Analysis template for you to complete. Use the worksheets you previously filled out to guide you, but feel free to add additional details or focus on the most important aspects for your law firm.

As you fill in the section listing your strengths, weaknesses, and special qualities, add in details about your competition. Perhaps you noticed a particular strength of yours that other law firms don't seem to have. Make a note of that. Or maybe there is a subsection of your practice area that other firms have a good grasp on, but that you need to understand better before you can advise clients. These details serve as reminders of how you can stay ahead of the competition in certain areas, and where you need to improve.

## BUSINESS PLAN: MARKET ANALYSIS

| Target Market | |
|---|---|

*(continued)*

**BUSINESS PLAN: MARKET ANALYSIS** *(continued)*

| Competitive Analysis | Strengths: |
|---|---|
| | Areas of Improvement: |
| | Special Qualities: |

As you fill out this portion of your business plan, be honest with yourself in both areas. "Anyone who pays" is not an ideal client, and you won't be able to focus your marketing efforts and draw in new business if you maintain such a broad, undefined scope of the people or businesses you serve.

You must also be really clear about what your strengths and weaknesses are. This will help you make educated decisions about how to grow your firm. It can affect the types of cases you take, who you hire, and the types of systems you set up. For example, if you know that you tend to procrastinate on big projects, include that as an area for improvement. Then create procedures that help reduce your procrastination. Maybe set up lots of reminders or give yourself a reward to work toward when you finish a project. Whatever your particular weaknesses are, having them in your business plan keeps you aware of them and able to focus on improvements.

## SECTION 4: MARKETING PLAN

The Marketing Plan section of your business plan is very important and will serve as your guide to attracting new clients to your firm. You don't want to be broke forever, right? In this section, you will create an actionable plan for marketing your business. You will think of different avenues for marketing, set guidelines for pursuing those avenues, and when you revisit your business plan in a few months, evaluate whether your plan is working and how you can improve it.

The marketing plan requires you to think creatively and look closely at the needs, wants, and interests of your specific target client. Use the Marketing Ideas worksheet to brainstorm potential areas where you can obtain business and how you can do it.

I will fill out a couple lines with examples to give you an idea, but think about community outreach, networking with attorneys and other professionals, social media, and word-of-mouth referrals. Refer back to Chapter 4, "Getting Clients," for a refresher on some of the best marketing techniques for new law firms.

## MARKETING IDEAS

| Referral Source | Marketing Activities | Goals |
|---|---|---|
| Past clients | Send handwritten birthday and holiday cards to past clients and their family members. | Send at least one card per quarter to each client. |
| Facebook | Engage with followers using Facebook Live; post relevant news articles; make the Facebook page interactive and interesting. | Do one half-hour Facebook Live post per week. |
| | | |
| | | |

(continued)

**MARKETING IDEAS** *(continued)*

| | | |
|---|---|---|
| | | |
| | | |
| | | |
| | | |
| | | |
| | | |

Marketing is an area that will constantly change as you learn more and make improvements in your business, so edit this section of your business plan regularly. Figure out what works, and stick to it and improve it. When something doesn't work, just pivot to something different.

Now that you have some ideas, it's time to draft the Marketing Plan section of your business plan. Tailor your plan to your needs, even changing the headings, but use the template to get you started.

**BUSINESS PLAN: MARKETING PLAN**

| | |
|---|---|
| **Introduction**<br>What are the two to three overarching strategies you will use to obtain new business? | |
| **Strategy #1:** ____________________<br>Fill in the first way you will focus your marketing efforts.<br>Write out, in detail, the specific actions you will take. | |
| **Strategy #2:** ____________________<br>Fill in the second way you will focus your marketing efforts.<br>Write out, in detail, the specific actions you will take. | |
| **Strategy #3:** ____________________<br>Fill in the third way you will focus your marketing efforts.<br>Write out, in detail, the specific actions you will take. | |

Base your marketing plan on your current situation and the different marketing options available to you. When I started my firm, Facebook Live was not yet available, but once I incorporated it into my marketing strategy, I went back and revised my business plan. Similarly, you should constantly review, adjust, and update your business plan to fit your needs at any given point in your firm.

# SECTION 5: OPERATIONS

The Operations section is the last substantive section of your business plan. However, it is packed full of the important, practical information about your business. Here, you will outline details about your office facilities, your staff, the equipment and furniture you own, your customer service guidelines, research and development, your technology plan, the financial structure of your firm, the management structure, and the development plan for your business. Whew, that's a lot!

Even though this section covers a lot of the drier information about your business, it is one of the most important sections for two reasons. First, it helps you keep an organized record of everything about your business. This is helpful for you as a business owner, and it is necessary in case something happens and someone outside the firm needs to take over, such as in the event of a serious accident or death. Second, if you ever decide to seek investors in your business, this section outlines much of the information investors will want to see. Overall, this section provides a detailed outline of the practical aspects of the operation of your firm.

## YOUR BUSINESS PLAN: OPERATIONS

| | |
|---|---|
| **Facilities**<br>In what geographical location is your office located?<br>What is the address?<br>What is the office setup?<br>Is the office located near any public transportation?<br>Is there parking near the office?<br>What is the proximity of the office to other locations you frequent in your business, such as the courthouse?<br>How much do you pay to rent your office?<br>What are the terms of your rental contract? | |
| **Staff**<br>Who do you employ?<br>What do you pay your staff members?<br>What are your staff members' responsibilities?<br>What are your staffing goals? | |
| **Equipment and Furniture**<br>List the following for all furniture and equipment you currently own:<br>• Description<br>• Purchase status (new or used)<br>• Purchase date<br>• Cost<br>• Payments<br>List the following for all furniture and equipment you currently lease:<br>• Description<br>• Lease status (new or used)<br>• Lease date<br>• Cost<br>• Payments | |

## YOUR BUSINESS PLAN: OPERATIONS *(continued)*

| | |
|---|---|
| List the following for all furniture and equipment you plan to purchase in the future:<br>• Description<br>• Purchase status (new or used)<br>• Projected purchase date<br>• Anticipated cost<br>• Anticipated payments<br>List the following for all furniture and equipment you plan to lease in the future:<br>• Description<br>• Purchase status (new or used)<br>• Projected purchase date<br>• Anticipated cost<br>• Anticipated payments | |
| **Customer Service**<br>What are your firm office hours?<br>How will you meet with clients (appointment only, walk-ins)?<br>What is your plan for responding to missed calls and emails?<br>What is your plan for updating clients about developments in their case? | |
| **Research and Development**<br>How will you conduct legal research?<br>What will you do to keep current with new developments in the law and community? | |
| **Technology Plan**<br>What type of technology will you use in your firm?<br>What email program will you use?<br>What phone company or program will you use?<br>What case management software will you use?<br>What accounting software will you use? | |
| **Financial Control**<br>Who will have financial control of the business?<br>Who can sign checks?<br>What types of accounts will the firm have?<br>What bank will manage your accounts?<br>What will you do if a client does not pay on time or at all? | |

*(continued)*

**YOUR BUSINESS PLAN: OPERATIONS** *(continued)*

| | |
|---|---|
| What accounting software will you use?<br>How will you stay on top of your income and expenses for tax purposes?<br>Who will prepare your taxes?<br>How will you protect your financial information? | |
| **Management**<br>What are your management needs?<br>If you have staff or managers:<br>• What are your management objectives?<br>• Who is on your management team?<br>• What are the management responsibilities?<br>• What are the necessary management qualifications?<br>• What is the compensation for managers? | |
| **Development Plan**<br>What is your mission statement?<br>What is your vision statement?<br>What is your top practice goal?<br>What are your strategies for accomplishing that goal?<br>What is your exit plan for dissolving the firm? | |

This is the last section of your business plan, so if you've made it this far, you're doing great. The next step is to take notes from the previous sections to create an executive summary. This will be much easier since you already did the heavy lifting.

## SECTION 1: EXECUTIVE SUMMARY (ROUND 2)

You've made it to Round 2 of the Executive Summary section. Congratulations, you're almost done with your business plan (insert party popper emoji here)![1]

The executive summary should include a company description, mission statement, goals, stage of development, practice areas, target market, competitors, competitive advantage, and your sales and advertising strategy. Essentially, you're just summarizing all the other sections into a quick introductory section that gives a snapshot of your business. Using the detailed analysis you went through in later sections of your business plan, fill in the following template to create the Executive Summary section of your business plan. Remember, this is the first thing people will see, so make sure it is concise but strong.

[1] Again, it would be too expensive to print a colorful party popper emoji, so I need you to use your imagination for me.

## YOUR BUSINESS PLAN: EXECUTIVE SUMMARY

| | |
|---|---|
| Company Description | |
| Mission Statement | |
| Goals | Immediate Goals:<br><br>Top Practice Goal: |
| Stage of Development | |
| Practice Areas | |
| Target Market | |
| Competitors | |
| Competitive Advantage | |
| Sales and Advertising Strategy | |

Congratulations! You have finished the first draft of your first business plan. Remember, your business plan is something you should constantly review and update. I try to update mine at least every six months, but once a year at a minimum. Set aside some time on the calendar now, so you remember to review in the future.

You can find a full business plan template in Appendix F. I also included a sample of my business plan from 2016 in Appendix G, so you can see what it looked like shortly after I started the firm. Use this as a guide as you create your business plan, but feel free to change things to best fit your needs.

If you are still looking for a comprehensive, focused guide, there is an excellent paper titled "Building a Great Business Plan for Your New Law Practice" by Freya Allan Shoffner, which you can find with a quick Google search. Many of the tips I outlined for you I originally discovered in this article and then supplemented with my own research.

## CHAPTER CHECKLIST: MAKE A PLAN

- ❒ **Create your business plan.** Use the examples provided and the template to fill in each section of the business plan. Refer back to earlier chapters for more details on information you will add to each section.
    - ❒ **Fill in the Basic Business Concept section.** This is where you go into the basics of your business. What type of law will you practice? Where are you located? Use the samples and templates to work through this.
    - ❒ **Fill in the Market Analysis section.** In this section, dig deep into your target market. To be successful, you need to know exactly who your audience is.
    - ❒ **Fill in the Marketing Plan section.** Now you get to outline your plan for targeting your ideal client. How are you going to reach this person or business? What actions do you need to take to ensure your ideal client finds and hires you?
    - ❒ **Fill in the Operations section.** This section outlines the boring, day-to-day stuff that is necessary for running a firm. Use the sample and template to go through this section.
    - ❒ **Create the executive summary.** Even though this gets placed at the beginning of the business plan, you will prepare it at the end, once you have all the nitty-gritty filled into the other sections.
- ❒ **Casually drop your business plan into conversation with other small law firm owners.** "I was just updating my business plan the other day, when . . ." or "Wow, this speaking opportunity sounds awesome! That will fit right into my business plan too." Watch their mouths drop and listen to them stammer as they realize what a badass business owner you are.

# Final Thoughts

Whether you've already opened your new law firm or you're planning to open it down the road, implementing the suggestions outlined in this book will ensure you are on the path to success. Read and reread this book, as needed. Fill out the worksheets and write in the margins. Note the things that have worked for you and those that need some tweaking. Your business is an evolving creature, so allow yourself to be flexible.

Before I set you free, let me give you the top eight tips I have learned in my five-plus years as a law firm owner:

1. Even after you start making money, pretend you're broke every time you make a purchase. Weigh the pros and cons, and ensure the value of the purchase outweighs the cost.
2. Start streamlining your business from Day 1, even if you don't have any staff. This will save you a ton of energy and time when you're ready to hire.
3. As soon as you start getting more work than you can handle by yourself, hire an assistant. It's really scary the first time, but completely worth it. And with the guide outlined in this book, you'll hire someone good.
4. Treat everybody you interact with as an attorney with respect (well really, treat everyone with respect). This includes your clients, staff, court administrators, help-desk operators, colleagues, and bank tellers. The nicer you are to people, the more likely they are to help you out in a bind.
5. Step outside the box. Find and regularly interact with other attorneys who are doing things differently. Learn from them, and be creative.
6. Cater to your clients' needs and your needs, and don't worry about what everyone around you thinks. Being a different, creative attorney often comes with some side-eye from those stuck inside the box. Expect it, embrace it, and know that you are doing the best for you.
7. Embrace social media marketing. Figure out where to find your ideal client on social media and be there as much as possible.
8. When you're feeling exceptionally tired and broke, know that you will get there. Just keep following the steps in this book and carefully watching your practice to see what is working and what isn't. Don't be afraid to make changes.

The idea of starting your own law firm is scary, but you have the tools to make it happen. Now you just need to take the leap! Think about what you truly want as an attorney, and then follow your gut. I have never been so fulfilled as I am running my own law firm, and I want you to have an equally amazing experience. Now go forth and kick ass!

# Appendix A
# Weekly Tasks

| | |
|---|---|
| Monday | ❒<br>❒<br>❒<br>❒ |
| Tuesday | ❒<br>❒<br>❒<br>❒ |
| Wednesday | ❒<br>❒<br>❒<br>❒ |
| Thursday | ❒<br>❒<br>❒<br>❒ |
| Friday | ❒<br>❒<br>❒<br>❒ |
| Saturday | ❒<br>❒<br>❒<br>❒ |
| Sunday | ❒<br>❒<br>❒<br>❒ |

# Appendix B

# Solo and Small Firm Procedures Checklist

### Daily

- ❒ Have I returned all telephone calls and responded to all pertinent emails?
- ❒ Have I recorded all my billable and nonbillable time?
- ❒ Have I recorded all new appointments, hearings, and events on my calendar?

### Weekly

- ❒ Have I recorded all of my travel time on my expenses sheet and MyCase client expenses?
- ❒ Have I reviewed and categorized my firm income and expenses?
- ❒ Have I reviewed all time entries for the week?
- ❒ Have I mailed a welcome letter with a magnet to all new clients?
- ❒ Have I followed up with last week's consultations?
- ❒ Have I sent invoices for all new contract work?
- ❒ Have I scheduled at least two networking/marketing luncheons/meetings for next week?
- ❒ Have I gone through my "For Fridays" email folder and resolved all emails?
- ❒ Is my computer data successfully backed up this week?
    - ❒ Are all incoming and outgoing documents properly filed in the clients' files?
    - ❒ Have I accounted for all of my time this week, and recorded it for billing my clients?
- ❒ What events are scheduled next week that need my attention today?
- ❒ Have I completed my scheduled marketing activities this week?

- ❒ Have I shared or commented on at least one item that is valuable to my target audience on my website, blog, or social media?
- ❒ Have I updated my contacts to include the new acquaintances I met this week and have I invited them to join my social media circles and/or accepted their requests to connect (i.e., LinkedIn)?

### Monthly

- ❒ Have I transferred 35 percent of my net income for the month into tax savings?
- ❒ Have I paid my business credit card?
- ❒ Have I transferred $2,000 into business savings?
- ❒ Have I mailed a case status and next steps letter to all clients with an update in their case?
- ❒ Have all my client bills been sent?
- ❒ Have I called everyone whose account is 45 days past due?
- ❒ Do I need to withdraw from any representation where the client has not paid?
- ❒ Have I contacted all of my clients this month (case update letter, phone call, meeting, etc.)?
- ❒ Have I restored a test file to make sure my computer backup worked?
- ❒ Are my computer security software and case management program up-to-date and running properly on all computers?
- ❒ Have I read at least one rule this month in the Rules of Professional Conduct?
- ❒ Have I thrown out all junk mail I haven't read from last month and deleted all unnecessary emails from my inbox?
- ❒ Are there any client files that can be closed, returned to the client, or placed in storage?
- ❒ Have I reconciled my trust account, comparing the ledger balances, checks, deposits, and bank statement? Have I filed these records for future use?
- ❒ Have I transferred earned fees from the client trust account to my operating account?
- ❒ Have we held a monthly office meeting to discuss administrative and legal issues important to staff members?

### Every Three Months

- ❒ Have I taken time out/scheduled a time to review all active physical files with the designated paralegal?

### Every Six Months

- ❒ Have I maintained my computer by cleaning out old documents and running regular utility programs?
- ❒ Have I taken time to review my business plan? How am I doing?
- ❒ Have I reviewed my office from a client's perspective? What can I do to improve it?
- ❒ Have I compared my projected budget to my actual expenses and income for the past six months? What changes do I need to make in my operating budget?

Some of these tasks can be delegated to staff, but do not abdicate your responsibility. Review the work to ensure it is completed correctly. After all, it is your business and your professional license.

## Appendix C

# Fee Tracking Spreadsheet

| CLIENT NAME | FEE STRUCTURE | TOTAL FEE | TOTAL PAID | NEXT PAYMENT AMOUNT | NEXT PAYMENT DUE |
|---|---|---|---|---|---|
| | | | | | |
| | | | | | |
| | | | | | |
| | | | | | |
| | | | | | |
| | | | | | |
| | | | | | |
| | | | | | |
| | | | | | |
| | | | | | |
| | | | | | |
| | | | | | |
| | | | | | |
| | | | | | |
| | | | | | |
| | | | | | |
| | | | | | |

## Appendix D

# Referral Tracking Spreadsheet—Consultations

| CONSULTS | MONTH | SOURCE | SOURCE | SOURCE | SOURCE | SOURCE | SOURCE | SOURCE |
|---|---|---|---|---|---|---|---|---|
| | January | | | | | | | |
| | February | | | | | | | |
| | March | | | | | | | |
| | April | | | | | | | |
| | May | | | | | | | |
| | June | | | | | | | |
| | July | | | | | | | |
| | August | | | | | | | |
| | September | | | | | | | |
| | October | | | | | | | |
| | November | | | | | | | |
| | December | | | | | | | |
| | Total | | | | | | | |

## REFERRAL TRACKING SPREADSHEET—NEW CLIENTS

| NEW CLIENTS | MONTH | SOURCE | SOURCE | SOURCE | SOURCE | SOURCE | SOURCE | SOURCE |
|---|---|---|---|---|---|---|---|---|
| | January | | | | | | | |
| | February | | | | | | | |
| | March | | | | | | | |
| | April | | | | | | | |
| | May | | | | | | | |
| | June | | | | | | | |
| | July | | | | | | | |
| | August | | | | | | | |
| | September | | | | | | | |
| | October | | | | | | | |
| | November | | | | | | | |
| | December | | | | | | | |
| | **Total** | | | | | | | |

## Appendix E

# Time Tracking Spreadsheet

| CLIENT NUMBER | CLIENT/ CASE NAME | DATE | SERVICES PERFORMED | TIME |
|---|---|---|---|---|
| | | | | |
| | | | | |
| | | | | |
| | | | | |
| | | | | |
| | | | | |
| | | | | |
| | | | | |
| | | | | |
| | | | | |
| | | | | |
| | | | | |
| | | | | |
| | | | | |
| | | | | |
| | | | | |
| | | | | |
| | | | | |
| | | | | |

# Appendix F
# Business Plan

Draft date:

## Executive Summary

### Company Description

### Mission Statement

### Goals

**Immediate goals:**

**Top practice goal:**

Stage of Development

Practice Areas

Target Market

Competitors

[Your Firm Name]'s Competitive Advantage

Sales and Advertising Strategy

## Basic Business Concept

[Insert introduction]

## Definition of Practice

Firm name:
Founding date:
Legal form:
State of establishment:
Owner:
Principal attorney:
Location:
Geographic area served:
Immediate goals:
Progress of current goals:

## Practice Area

# Market Analysis

## Target Market

**Primary Target Market:**

**Secondary Target Market:**

## Competitive Analysis

**Strengths:**

**Areas of Improvement:**

## Marketing Plan

[First Marketing Strategy]

[Second Marketing Strategy]

[Third Marketing Strategy]

## Operations

Facilities

Staff

## Equipment and Furniture

Currently Owned Furniture and Equipment

| DESCRIPTION | SKU NUMBER | PURCHASE STATUS | DATE PURCHASED | COST | PAYMENTS | EMPLOYEE IN POSSESSION OF EQUIPMENT |
|---|---|---|---|---|---|---|
| | | | | | | |
| | | | | | | |
| | | | | | | |
| | | | | | | |
| | | | | | | |
| | | | | | | |
| | | | | | | |
| | | | | | | |

Currently Leased Furniture and Equipment

| DESCRIPTION | SKU NUMBER | PURCHASE STATUS | DATE PURCHASED | COST | PAYMENTS | EMPLOYEE IN POSSESSION OF EQUIPMENT |
|---|---|---|---|---|---|---|
| | | | | | | |
| | | | | | | |
| | | | | | | |
| | | | | | | |
| | | | | | | |
| | | | | | | |
| | | | | | | |
| | | | | | | |

Customer Service

Research and Development

Technology Plan

Financial Control

Management

Development Plan

**Mission Statement**:

**Vision Statement**:

**Top Practice Goal**:

**Exit Plan**:

# Appendix G

# Sample Business Plan for Eagan Immigration

Draft date: February 12, 2016

## OUTLINE

*Customer Service*
*Research and Development*
*Technology Plan*
*Financial Control*
*Management*
*Development Plan*

## Executive Summary

### Company Description

Eagan Immigration is an immigration law firm. It is a sole proprietorship owned by Lauren Eagan and has two locations, one in Washington, DC, and one in Tyson's Corner, VA.

### Mission Statement

To provide immigrants with a safe environment to learn about their immigration options and obtain the benefits for which they qualify.

### Goals

**Immediate goals:** Build client base: Retain 4 new clients each month in 2016.
**Top practice goal**: Eagan Immigration's main goal is to become a leader in immigration law. Eagan Immigration's name will be well-known and respected, and it will dominate competitors in collections. After five years, Eagan Immigration will retain an average of $30,000 in new business per month. Eagan Immigration's founder will earn at least $120,000 per year and will be asked to speak at an AILA National Conference at least three times between 2015 and 2019. Eagan Immigration will have a staff of one to two legal assistants and one associate attorney.

### Stage of Development

Eagan Immigration began operations in October 2014. It uses a virtual office space on an as-needed basis, and it receives all mail at that address. Eagan Immigration currently has 28 active cases and 12 closed cases. The founding attorney, Lauren Eagan, has spoken at multiple events in the community about immigration law issues, volunteers weekly at a legal clinic, and attends approximately two networking events per week. Eagan Immigration is also active on social media and has a well-designed website.

### Practice Areas

Eagan Immigration practices immigration law exclusively. It handles all types of immigration law cases, including removal defense litigation, family-based immigration, complex citizenship and naturalization, relief for victims of violence or abuse, and employment-based immigration.

## Target Market

Immigrants in the DC Metro areas, with a focus on Spanish-speaking immigrants.

## Competitors

There are multiple immigration law firms throughout the DC Metro area, the majority of which are small- to medium-sized law firms with fewer than ten attorneys. However, members of many of these law firms work together informally and regularly refer business to one another.

## Eagan Immigration's Competitive Advantage

Eagan Immigration's founding attorney, Lauren Eagan, is fluent in Spanish and plans to hire only Spanish-speaking staff as the firm grows. This gives Eagan Immigration a competitive advantage with the Spanish-speaking immigrant population. Eagan Immigration also offers competitive fees and is more affordable than many of the well-established immigration law firms in the area. Additionally, Eagan Immigration is located near the Metro Center, which is easily accessible to most metro lines.

## Sales and Advertising Strategy

Eagan Immigration plans to obtain business based on word-of-mouth referrals. To begin promoting Eagan Immigration, the firm took multiple cases on a pro bono basis, so that clients could interact with the firm. The firm still occasionally takes pro bono cases, and Lauren Eagan volunteers at the St. Anthony's Parish Legal Clinic, where she consults with multiple potential clients weekly. Lauren Eagan is also active in multiple networking groups and attends approximately two networking events per week. The firm is present on social media and posts articles on all of its accounts and its website about three times per week. Lauren Eagan also writes and publishes immigration-related articles, which the firm publicizes through its social media accounts. Lauren Eagan also records informational videos, which she posts on YouTube. The firm receives approximately three to five emails per day from people who viewed these videos, and multiple viewers have paid for consultations with Lauren Eagan.

# Basic Business Concept

There is a substantial need for a law firm that addresses the immigration law needs of the Spanish-speaking immigrant population in the DC Metro area. Eagan Immigration will serve both individuals and businesses with their immigration needs. Its focus will be on representing clients in removal proceedings in immigration court, family-based immigration, clients with complex criminal and/or immigration histories, and complex citizenship and naturalization cases. Eagan Immigration will also serve immigrants who are victims of abuse, violence, or trauma.

Eagan Immigration will develop business primarily through word-of-mouth referrals. Eagan Immigration will volunteer with nonprofit organizations to develop relationships with other attorneys and potential clients there. It will handle multiple cases on a pro bono basis at any given time, in order to develop relationships with new clients who could become the source of future paying referrals. Eagan Immigration attorneys will regularly host, provide legal services at, and give presentations at community workshops, clinics, and events as a way to maintain exposure within the immigrant community. Eagan Immigration attorneys will also regularly attend networking events and trainings with other attorneys who could become referral sources.

Although there are many successful immigration law firms in the DC Metro area, Eagan Immigration has several competitive advantages. First, while the founding attorney has significant experience working for a large immigration firm and handling complex immigration issues, clients will receive the personalized attention of a small firm. Clients will develop a relationship with their attorney and communicate directly with her, rather than working only with paralegals and other staff. And Eagan Immigration's attorneys will always respond to client messages promptly, typically within one business day. Second, Eagan Immigration's founding attorney is fluent in Spanish. Eagan Immigration plans to hire only Spanish-speaking individuals as the firm grows, in order to best serve the Spanish-speaking immigrant population. And third, Eagan Immigration's office is centrally located in Washington, DC, only half a block from the Metro Center. This location provides easy access to clients from DC, Maryland, and Virginia.

## Definition of Practice

| | |
|---|---|
| Firm name: | Eagan Immigration |
| Founding date: | October 23, 2014 |
| Legal form: | PLLC |
| State of establishment: | District of Columbia |
| Owner: | Lauren A. Eagan, Esq. |
| Principal attorney: | Lauren A. Eagan, Esq. |
| Location: | 1325 G Street NW, Ste. 500, Washington, DC 20005 |
| Geographic area served: | DC Metro Area |
| Immediate goals: | Build client base. Retain four new clients each month in Q1 2016. |
| Progress of current goals: | |

## Practice Area

The practice area is immigration law, and the firm will focus on two primary subsets of that practice area, family-based immigration and removal defense litigation. About

15 years ago, immigration laws in the United States were far less stringent, and many individuals who were deported from the United States easily re-entered unlawfully. Because it was easy to reenter the United States, many individuals failed to take the proper steps to legalize themselves or their family members. Therefore, many individuals now have complex immigration histories due to mistakes they or their parents made years ago. Additionally, individuals failed to fight their removal cases, even if they qualified for a defense to removal. As a result, many people have one or multiple deportation orders, which bar them from immigration benefits. And as immigration laws have tightened over the last 15 years, so have removals. Now, individuals who were never removal priorities are being arrested and detained. It is much more difficult for undocumented immigrants to remain "in the shadows." Therefore, because immigration laws have tightened over the past 15 years, it is much more difficult for individuals to enter and remain in the United States unlawfully, and the need for quality immigration legal services has increased.

# Market Analysis

## Target Market

**Primary target market:** Immigrant families and individuals, particularly Spanish-speakers, who have a high school education or less, work in low-level jobs, and have an annual household income of approximately $60,000 or less. Serious clients that are willing to invest in their case. Not internet savvy.

**Secondary target market**: Immigrant individuals who have a college education, work in well-established companies, and have an individual income of at least $50,000.

## Competitive Analysis

After reviewing the practices of other immigration law firms in the DC Metro area, Eagan Immigration has many strengths, as well as specific areas of improvement:

**Strengths:** Eagan Immigration has several competitive advantages over its competition. First, Eagan Immigration attorneys have a high level of experience, especially when compared to many of the newer immigration law practices in the area. Eagan Immigration also offers competitive pricing and payment plan options for clients. And Eagan Immigration attorneys are fluent in Spanish, allowing Eagan Immigration to target the Spanish-speaking community.

Additionally, Eagan Immigration covers a wide range of immigration law issues. It is efficient and flexible to client needs. Former clients of Eagan Immigration describe the attorney as helpful, kind, responsive, hard-working, and a "miracle worker." As Eagan Immigration grows, it should strive to maintain these characteristics.

**Areas of improvement:** Eagan Immigration has minimal experience in business immigration. This puts the firm at a disadvantage in this specific subarea of immigration law. To improve in this area, Eagan Immigration plans to attend trainings and events targeted at business immigration. Eagan Immigration attorneys should also read business immigration guides to familiarize themselves with the different immigrant and nonimmigrant visa options for potential clients. The firm should also take on business immigration cases pro bono or on a low-fee basis in order to gain more experience in this area of immigration law.

Eagan Immigration also has some other areas of improvement, such as strengthening attention to detail and procrastinating on large projects. Eagan Immigration attorneys should review their work product multiple times, in online format and print format, before submitting it. When an attorney receives a new case, the attorney should begin work immediately, and set internal deadlines for various steps of the case. The attorney should stick to those deadlines, rather than pushing them back to make room for other projects.

If Eagan Immigration can make these suggested improvements, it will gain an even greater competitive advantage in the field of immigration law.

## Marketing Plan

### Client Retention

Eagan Immigration has identified two primary outlets for obtaining new clients: (1) word-of-mouth referrals from past clients, current clients, and other members in the community and (2) referrals from other attorneys. To increase word-of-mouth referrals, Eagan Immigration will focus on creating and maintaining positive relationships with past and current clients and increasing involvement and visibility in the immigrant community. To increase referrals from attorneys, Eagan Immigration will actively network in the legal community. Eagan Immigration will focus on the following advertising efforts for 2016:

### Word-of-Mouth Referrals

Client Relationships:

- Mail case status letters to all current clients monthly
- Call all current clients to discuss case status monthly
- Mail a thank-you letter with case outline and an Eagan Immigration magnet to new clients after Eagan Immigration is retained
- Mail handwritten cards to all clients, spouses, and children on their birthdays
- Mail handwritten year-end holiday cards
- Mail a thank-you card and gift card to clients who refer other clients resulting in a consultation
- Mail periodic newsletters to past and current clients

Community Outreach:

- Volunteer at Saint Anthony's Legal Clinic weekly
- Participate in community volunteer events, as available

Social Media:

- Create and post one informational YouTube video per month
- Post three articles to Facebook, LinkedIn, Twitter, and Google+ per week
- Post all new weekly articles on the Eagan Immigration website once per week
- Post client testimonials on the Eagan Immigration website and encourage clients to post the testimonial on Facebook at the conclusion of every case
- Encourage clients to follow Eagan Immigration on social media
- Eagan Immigration social media advertising campaign that targets potential clients
- Host monthly radio-style phone call to which potential clients can call-in and ask questions

Follow up with all potential clients that called into the phone call

<u>Attorney Referrals</u>

Networking:

- Attend two networking events per week
- Maintain an active membership and regularly participate in the following organizations:
  - American Immigration Lawyers Association (AILA)
  - Women's Bar Association of DC (WBAC)
- Maintain the following leadership position:
  - AILA New Member Division Committee Member
- Maintain positive continuing relationships with attorneys who repeatedly refer clients
  - Mail a thank-you card and gift card to clients who refer other clients resulting in a consultation

Professional Outreach:

- Conduct 2 AILA webinars per year
- Speak on panel at AILA National Conference
- Eagan Immigration is open to writing articles when asked by a reputable organization

# Operations

## Facilities

Eagan Immigration has two office locations in the DC Metro area. The primary location is located at 1325 G Street NW, Suite 500, Washington, DC 20005. The secondary location is located at 1750 Tysons Blvd, Suite 1500, McLean, VA 22102. These buildings are shared office spaces with a common reception area. They are professionally decorated and made up of multiple offices that can either be leased long-term or hourly. The second location was added to be more convenient for clients from Virginia to access; it gives clients who would not have been able to meet in the Washington, DC, location another option.

The Washington, DC, office is centrally located to service clients in Washington, DC; Virginia; and Maryland. It is approximately 20 minutes from the Immigration Court in Arlington and approximately 1 hour from the Immigration Court in Baltimore. It is located less than one block from the Metro Center metro stop, which is accessible by multiple metro lines. Clients can also pay for parking in various garages nearby, including the office building's garage, or pay meters to park on the street.

The Tysons Corner, VA, office is centrally located to service clients in northern Virginia. It is approximately 15 minutes from the Immigration Court in Arlington and approximately 1 hour from the Immigration Court in Baltimore. It is located two blocks from the Tysons Corner metro stop, which is accessible by the Silver line, and a bus stop. Clients can also park in the office building parking lot for $3.00 per hour.

Eagan Immigration has a lease with Carr Workplaces which permits 16 hours of individual office use at the Virginia location, at a rate of $200.00 per month. The lease allows for the Washington, DC, location to be rented at a rate of $20 per hour. Additionally, Eagan Immigration pays $99.00 per month for a mailbox at the Virginia location and $86.90 per month at the Washington, DC, location. Eagan Immigration may cancel this agreement with 30 days' notice. Eagan Immigration can, at any time, increase this plan to include more time individual office use. Furthermore, Carr Workplaces offers full-time office spaces at both locations, so Eagan Immigration could expand into a permanent office in the future, as the firm grows.

## Staff

In addition to the founding attorney, Eagan Immigration has one administrative assistant staff member who was hired in February 2016. The administrative assistant is responsible for both administrative and paralegal activities as directed by the principal attorney. With the addition of the administrative assistant, the founding attorney can focus on complex legal work and business development. By the end of 2016, Eagan Immigration plans to hire a full-time associate attorney. As the firm continues to grow, more employees may be required. Eagan Immigration will analyze its staffing needs quarterly.

## Equipment and Furniture

### Currently Owned Furniture and Equipment

| Description | Purchase Status | Date Purchased | Cost | Payments |
|---|---|---|---|---|
| Surface Pro 3 | New | 12/7/15 | $750 | Paid |
| Epson WD-4530 Printer | New | 4/10/13 | $300 | Paid |
| Plastic Filing Cabinet | New | 10/18/14 | $30 | Paid |
| Samsung Galaxy S6 Cell Phone | New | 1/2/11 | $550 | Paid |
| WD External Hard Drive | | | | |
| Thumb Drive | | | | |
| Asus Laptop | New | 1/2/11 | $550 | Paid |
| Epson WD Printer | New | 1/2/11 | $550 | Paid |

### Currently Leased Furniture and Equipment

| Description | Status | Date Purchased | Cost | Payments |
|---|---|---|---|---|
| None | | | | |

### Furniture and Equipment to Purchase

| Description | Status | Purchase By Date | Anticipated Cost | Anticipated Payments |
|---|---|---|---|---|
| Sturdy Filing Cabinet | Used | 06/01/16 | $50 | None |
| Small Bookshelf | Used | 06/01/16 | $30 | None |
| Trays for Stacking | New | 06/01/16 | $40 | None |
| Paper Shredder | New | 06/01/16 | $200 | None |
| Scanner | New | 06/01/16 | $250 | None |

### Furniture and Equipment to Lease

| Description | Status | Purchase By Date | Anticipated Cost | Anticipated Payments |
|---|---|---|---|---|
| None | | | | |

## Customer Service

Eagan Immigration will meet with clients and answer phone calls from 9:00 a.m. to 5:00 p.m., Monday through Friday. Client meetings are by appointment only. Eagan Immigration will respond to missed calls and client emails within one business day. Eagan Immigration attorneys will contact clients immediately with any major news or updates about their case.

## Research and Development

Eagan Immigration attorneys will use AILALink as its primary legal search engine. They will also conduct research by visiting the websites of various nonprofit organizations and legal research organizations and reviewing their recently posted practice advisories, unpublished cases, and country conditions reports. Eagan Immigration attorneys will also frequently review the websites of USCIS and EOIR for any changes in filing procedures.

In addition to case research, Eagan Immigration attorneys will strive to remain abreast of changes in case law and new forms of immigration relief. Attorneys will attend legal trainings in the community, with a goal of attending at least one immigration-related legal training per month. Attorneys will also maintain a strong network of other immigration attorneys in order to refer to their knowledge and experience. Attorneys will develop this network by regularly participating in AILA events and reviewing and posting information in the Cool Immigration Lawyers (CIL) group on Facebook. Attorneys are expected to attend at least one AILA event per month.

## Technology Plan

Eagan Immigration will strive to maintain a virtual office, and all technology will be accessible online. This will allow Eagan Immigration to access cases from any location on any computer.

Eagan Immigration will maintain a Google account, and each attorney and staff member will receive an individual email address associated with the account. This email address will give them access to other Google programs used by Eagan Immigration. Eagan Immigration's phone lines will route through Google Voice, and all missed calls and messages will record in Eagan Immigration's Google Voice account. Staff members will also be able to quickly communicate with one another with Google Hangouts.

Eagan Immigration will use Google products for drafting legal work, storing files, and maintaining client records. It will use Google Drive to store client files, and will only retain paper files for original documents or documents to be imminently filed. Eagan Immigration will record all client contact information on Google Contacts. It will prepare all written work in Google Docs. In order to comply with ethical rules, Eagan Immigration will maintain a copy of all case files on all firm computers as backup.

Additionally, Eagan Immigration will use online software for other business needs. It will use Wave for accounting. It will use AILALink for legal research. In general, Eagan Immigration will strive to keep all necessary software online only.

## Financial Control

Lauren Eagan, Founder and Managing Attorney, will retain primary financial control of Eagan Immigration. She is responsible for accounts payable and has the power of signature on all checks. Eagan Immigration has established a Business Checking Account, an IOLTA Account, and a credit card with Bank of America. Lauren Eagan will review these accounts for errors weekly. She will also make all final decisions regarding attorney fees and payment plans for clients.

Clients will be able to pay fees with cash, check, or credit card. Clients may make credit card payments using PayPal on Eagan Immigration's website. Client bills that are overdue more than 30 days will be charged interest of 10% APR. If a client has not paid his or her fees after 30 days, Eagan Immigration may terminate representation in the case. Where the client still refuses to pay, Eagan Immigration may use a collection agency to collect on overdue bills or file suit against the client, at the discretion of Lauren Eagan.

Eagan Immigration will use Wave for its accounting needs. Lauren Eagan will review all transactions in Wave weekly and categorize them. She will also document all purchases not recorded on Wave (including mileage expenses) in a separate spreadsheet on a weekly basis.

As a sole proprietor, Eagan Immigration is not required to file business taxes. However, Lauren Eagan will file a personal expected tax return quarterly. Eagan Immigration has retained Mike ABC of XXX firm to prepare quarterly and annual taxes for Eagan Immigration. Eagan Immigration hired ADP for payroll. They handle payroll and payroll taxes.

Eagan Immigration will protect its financial information by requiring a password to enter all firm computers, requiring a password to enter all bank accounts and accounting software, and locking the office.

## Management

At the time of establishment, Eagan Immigration does not have any managers or management needs apart from the sole proprietor, Lauren Eagan. As the firm grows and management needs arise, Eagan Immigration will review and complete the following objectives:

- Establish Eagan Immigration's management objectives
- Describe Eagan Immigration's management team
- Describe management responsibilities
- Define necessary management qualifications
- Management compensation

## Development Plan

**Mission statement:** To provide immigrants with a safe environment to learn about their immigration options and obtain the benefits for which they qualify.

**Vision statement:** To be a respected immigration law firm that clients view as honest and successful and that other attorneys contact for advice and to participate in speaking engagements.

**Top practice goal:** Eagan Immigration's main goal is to become a leader in immigration law. Eagan Immigration's name will be well-known and respected, and it will dominate competitors in collections. After five years, Eagan Immigration will retain an average of $30,000 in new business per month. Eagan Immigration's Founder will earn at least $120,000 per year and will be asked to speak at an AILA National Conference at least three times between 2015 and 2019. Eagan Immigration will have a staff of one to two legal assistants and one associate attorney. To achieve these goals, Eagan Immigration will use the following strategies:

- Promote Eagan Immigration
  - Attend at least one networking event per week
  - Volunteer at St. Anthony's weekly
  - Post to social media three times per week
  - Post a YouTube video once per month
- Develop a repeat client base
  - Volunteer at St. Anthony's weekly
  - Respond to client communications within one business day
  - Contact clients on the birthdays and holidays
  - Contact all current clients at least once monthly
- Consistently increase cash flow
  - Stick to set legal fees
  - Review set legal fees every six months and compare them with time spent on each type of case—increase fees if necessary
  - Set up reasonable payment plans for clients
  - Follow up with clients as soon as they miss a payment
  - Email or mail out all client bills monthly
  - Keep firm overhead as low as possible
- Develop respect in the legal community
  - Speak at one legal conference, event, or training per quarter
  - Post intelligent responses to questions on Cool Immigration Lawyers group on Facebook
  - Take on leadership roles in AILA
  - Regularly attend AILA events
- Win cases
  - Create a case plan immediately after taking case
  - Set internal deadlines for each case

- Use attention to detail in everything, from legal writing to procedural requirements
- Read Cool Immigration Lawyers posts, articles, and new cases

**Exit plan**: When Lauren Eagan is ready to dissolve Eagan Immigration, she will do so by minimizing her case load over a period of time. As she begins the process, she will only take new short-term cases and continue work on existing cases. When she is ready to completely close Eagan Immigration, she will stop taking new cases altogether. She will work on existing cases until they are all completed, at which time she will close Eagan Immigration.

If Lauren Eagan must leave Eagan Immigration quickly, she will sell her practice to a colleague. In this case, she will ensure that her clients will receive the same attention and quality of service that they received at Eagan Immigration. She will also make sure that the purchasing attorney is covered by malpractice insurance.

# Index